Those Things Which Are Above

THE HISTORY OF
ST. JOHN'S SCHOOL
LEATHERHEAD

Those Things Which Are Above

THE HISTORY OF
ST. JOHN'S SCHOOL
LEATHERHEAD

RICHARD HUGHES

GRESHAM BOOKS LTD
in partnership with
ST. JOHN'S SCHOOL, LEATHERHEAD

Published by
Gresham Books Limited
The Gresham Press
46 Victoria Road
Summertown
Oxford OX2 7QD

in partnership with

St. John's School, Leatherhead
Epsom Road
Leatherhead
Surrey
KT22 8SP

ISBN 0 946095 43 4

Design and typesetting by John Saunders Design & Production
Printed and bound by MPG Books Ltd, Bodmin, Cornwall

Acknowledgements

It is a daunting prospect to begin to thank the many people who have helped in the production of this book. I apologise in advance for those whose support goes unrecognised – I am certain to have forgotten someone. I should also emphasise that mention here does not constitute any responsibility for the reliability of the text – any inaccuracies are entirely my own. I would like to thank: Mrs. Evelyn Cowie, formerly of King's College, London, for encouraging me to embark upon the early history of the school; the Reverend Donald Aird and the Reverend John Barrie of St. Mark's, Hamilton Terrace; The Reverend John Walker of St. John's, Walworth; many members of the St. John's School community past and present, particularly Jessica Belfrage, Jimmy Bevan, Bill Chubb, Michael Comer, Fr. Matthew Lawson, Jack Stuttard and Pat Webb; J.E. Barnwell (of the Rutty family); Dr. Melvin Brooks; the Gordon Clark family and Jenny and Chris Ellins whose delightful Suffolk home offered sanctuary when deadlines loomed; Sally Todd, whose advice and expertise, particularly with illustrations, were invaluable; and a particular mention for Heather Adams and Judy Quick whose patience with my handwritten scrawl was saintly. Two Sixth Form students gave considerable help in the research – Jessica Hart and Edward Cole.

RBH

Contents

CHAPTER ONE

The Beginning

THE FOUNDER OF ST. JOHN'S SCHOOL, LEATHERHEAD, will remain an enigma. His name was Ashby Blair Haslewood and it would seem his weaknesses of character outweighed his strengths. Yet it was his inspiration which established the school. He is an unsung founder. There is no indication of his existence anywhere in the school today. No portrait of him hangs in public rooms; there is no Haslewood House, no Founder's Day; he does not even have a cup named after him. The reason for this will become apparent but it is important that the history of St. John's School begins with the person whose initiative set it in motion.

In 1851 Ashby Haslewood had been vicar of St. Mark's, Hamilton Terrace in the Marylebone district of London for four years. He was in fact the first incumbent of St. Mark's for the church had only completed its construction in 1847. He was, in 1851, forty years of age with a wife and child. A graduate of Christ's College, Cambridge, he had served as a deacon in Rochester and a curate in Greenwich before his appointment to St. Mark's. Ashby Haslewood in fact never lived in his parish – preferring an apartment in New Bond Street, Mayfair. This fact, amongst many others, was to create difficulties in the parish. Soon into his ministry he appointed a curate, Anthony Thomson, and it was he who resided in the parish in a substantial house close to the church. In this house St. John's School was to find its first location when its original pupils, eight eight-year-old boys, walked through its door in January 1852.

In October 1851 Ashby Haslewood sent out a letter to his parishioners. He had been at St. Mark's four years now and was keen both to establish an impressive choir and to set up a charitable institution in the name of the parish. Unfortunately the vicar's many enemies believed he had less impressive motives too. Anyway, the letter was distributed. 'I believe it is a source of regret that there has not hitherto been any charitable foundation connected with St. Mark's and I feel sure that parishioners would welcome the establishment of such a one as would offer a favourable exercise of their Christian sympathy and liberality.' He went on to propose the establishment of a school which would offer 'first-rate boarding, free of all charge, to the sons of clergymen with small incomes.' He then said that boys accepted into the school would be required to sing in the parish choir.

The idea was well received by the wealthy parishioners of Hamilton Terrace and funds were soon forthcoming. 'St. John's Foundation School for the Sons of Poor Clergy' opened its doors to its first pupils in January 1852. The eight boys were taught by the curate of St. Mark's, Anthony Thomson, who was the first Headmaster of the School. In fact Anthony Thomson was already coaching a handful of private pupils and the first St. John's boys were simply added to this group. One of the small group of pupils already being taught by Anthony Thomson was the son of a local musician; he was called Robert Romer and he grew up to be a Lord Justice of Appeal and a Privy Councillor. He has sometimes been cited as the first distinguished 'O.J.' but this is not strictly true – he was not the son of a clergyman and he was not one of the eight pupils who came to St. Mark's as part of Ashby Haslewood's charitable foundation. The phrase 'sons of poor clergy' is one that echoes through the history of the School, so we need to consider why these children were seen as objects of charitable concern.

When Ashby Haslewood sent out his letter to parishioners he was doing so in the midst of the mid-Victorian expansion of public school education when there was a large-scale establishment of new schools and a transformation of others designed to provide an education for the prospering professional classes. Between 1843 and 1853 at least ten schools regarded as 'major' public schools by 1900 were founded as well as many others of lesser status. In 1848 Nathaniel Woodard had published his pamphlet 'A Plea For The Middle Classes' where he had proposed 'a hierarchy of schools which should meet the needs of the different levels of the middle section of society.' At the time of Ashby Haslewood's letter Woodard had established his school for the second level of the middle-classes (tradesmen, farmers and the like) at Hurstpierpoint in Sussex. Soon afterwards another clergyman, J. L. Brereton, began his scheme of county schools, the two most successful of which, Cranleigh and Framlingham, were established in 1863 and 1864 respectively.

In this period of intense activity surrounding the provision of middle-class education there was a concern about the clergyman. Several of the schools emerging during the mid-Victorian boom offered generous provision for the education of clergy sons – either being specifically founded for the purpose (Marlborough, 1843, or Rossall, 1846) or, once established, developing generous schemes for clergy sons (Bradfield, 1850, and Malvern, 1865). The education of the clergy sons occupied the minds and pockets of many. Haslewood was not breaking new ground – indeed references to Marlborough and Rossall were made when he first appealed for donors. There was, though, a unique aspect to Haslewood's project – for he sought to provide a *free* education with board and lodging and he claimed no other school provided such generous provision for clergy sons, though clergy daughters did receive free schooling at St. Mary's Hall, Brighton.

The generosity of the first donors to St. John's would indicate that Ashby Haslewood had tapped into an area of charitable concern. The fact that many similar ventures were developing around the same time would confirm this. Many saw the inability of the clergyman to educate his own son in the middle-class manner as symbolic of the decline of the cleric. There was a political opposition to the influence of the Anglican church – an opposition strengthened by the 1851 religious census which suggested that the church no longer represented the views of the majority of Englishmen. In addition there was a more practical problem for the clergy – its increasing financial vulnerability. This vulnerability was the consequence of declining private sources of revenue, the selling off of land attached to parishes and the creation of poorly endowed new parishes.

The significance of 1851 must be mentioned. It was the year of the Great Exhibition. As Ashby Haslewood was establishing his school, London was packed with visitors – six million of them – who came to see the glorious Crystal Palace at Hyde Park, just the other end of the Edgware Road from Hamilton Terrace. The upper and middle classes of Britain were showing off – and they had cause. Three years earlier rebellion had erupted across Europe in the year of revolutions, 1848. Sufficient time had now elapsed for thought to be given as to why Britain had been spared such upheaval; some looked to the church as the provider of social and political cement. The prosperous classes of Britain were in proud mood in 1851 but many of their number were also reflective; the church was an institution vital for stability but it could not be taken for granted.

The financial precariousness of the clergyman was brought into sharp focus because the professions were flourishing and it was particularly noticeable when it came to the payment of fees at the expanding public schools. Increasingly these schools were becoming the schools of the professional classes yet a financial barrier prevented the clergy from sending their sons to them. The appeal which appeared each year in the early Annual Reports of the School sums up the situation:

'The social position of the clergy requires of them to preserve a decent exterior. The poor are accustomed to look to them for aid in their temporal as well in their spiritual need . . . Few cases are more pitiable than that of a parochial clergyman unable to provide for the necessities of himself and those dependent on him. For while he feels specially bound, as a teacher of morality to others, to set a high example of integrity, he is sometimes irresistibly drawn into pecuniary embarrassments which embitter his life and mar his usefulness . . . Among the many anxieties which press upon him, the want of a suitable education for his sons is one of the most deeply felt. Engaged constantly in the work of raising the moral and intellectual tone of others, he must needs grieve at the thought that his own children must, for the want of a proper education, sink in the social scale, the duties of his profession preventing him from giving them any but elementary instruction.'

There is no doubt the plight of the clergy was regarded as a major issue in the middle of the nineteenth century. In 1864 nineteen different charities for the poor clergy were founded in London alone. We know that the Bishop of London, the energetic and influential Charles Blomfield, did not encourage the establishment of St. John's because, amongst several misgivings, he argued that yet another charity for the clergy would dilute the funds available. It should be mentioned here that one of the reasons why the Bishop of London was less than enthusiastic about the founding of St. John's was that there had recently been established in a neighbouring area of North London the Clergy Orphan School. In 1852 the Clergy Orphan School received a donation allowing it to move to Canterbury – it became St. Edmund's, Canterbury – so St. John's ceased to pose a threat. One of the reasons Ashby Haslewood made all potential St. John's boys take a voice test for the choir was to allay the fears of the Bishop of London – to the Bishop he needed to give the impression that he was not adding to the long list of clergy charities but was simply looking for talented choirboys.

So there was certainly seen to be a problem with the consequence that St. John's became generously funded and had the opportunity for rapid expansion; eight pupils in 1852 became fifty by 1860.

But how poor were these 'poor clergy'? The committee published the financial circumstances of a selection of parents each year in the Annual Report. In 1857 the average parent earned £131; at the same time a semi-skilled worker's average pay was £50 per annum – a skilled worker's was £70 per annum. So the Johnian parent was considerably better off than a skilled or semi-skilled worker. But the Johnian parent would see himself as a professional person. The Headmaster of St. John's in the early 1860s, Edwards Hawkins, earned £322 per annum – and in addition he was allowed to supplement his income with private tuition. The 'third master', however, earned only £80 per annum but with free board and lodging. So the Johnian parent was considerably poorer than the Headmaster but a little better off than the average schoolmaster. It must be added, however, that Johnian parents in these early years seem to have put extra pressures on financial vulnerability through their fecundity: the first pupils of the School had an average of six brothers or sisters each. The payment of school fees for one or two children might have been manageable – but not five, six or seven. The idea of getting at least one child away to a school in London with free board and lodging must have appealed to the financially pressed clergyman.

So Ashby Blair Haslewood's great idea became a reality. St. John's School was founded in 1851 and its eight pupils sat down for their first lesson in January 1852.

CHAPTER TWO

'The Peculiar Circumstances of St. Mark's'

'MOST THINGS DONE BY ME ARE ATTRIBUTED TO A sordid motive.' This was the poignant answer Ashby Haslewood gave when asked to mention anything which caused problems for him in his parish. St. Mark's was subjected to a Visitation in 1858 – an inspection from the Bishop – and during its course the question was put to him: 'Can you mention anything which impedes your Ministry?' Ashby Haslewood's response had been frank.

Unfortunately St. John's School was one of the several ventures Ashby Haslewood was involved in which prompted suspicion from his parishioners and eventually from his Bishop and his M.P. It is hardly surprising, then, that soon after St. John's School was started several members of the committee – a committee Ashby Haslewood had reluctantly established on the insistence of the Bishop – began to seek ways of separating the school from its founder. A phrase taken from the report of the 1858 Visitation neatly sums up the problem – 'the peculiar circumstances of St. Mark's.' What were the 'peculiar circumstances'? Why was Ashby Haslewood so reviled?

To deal first with 'the peculiar circumstances': the land upon which St. Mark's was built was bought from the governors of Harrow School for £600. The person to whom the land was sold was Haslewood, at the time a curate at Greenwich. In other words the vicar purchased *himself* the land on which his church was built. With the land purchased, four trustees were appointed to supervise the finance and construction of the church; the four men were Charles Calley, Henry East – both early members of the St. John's committee – James Ponsford and Haslewood. The erection of the church building cost in excess of £7,000, so the cost of land and building was nearly £8,000. Of this, £4,000 'was temporarily furnished or supplied by Haslewood out of his own monies upon an understanding or agreement which was come to between Mr. Calley, Mr. East, Mr. Ponsford and Mr. Haslewood.'[1] The remaining money was raised from subscriptions and donations. It was agreed by the trustees that the £4,000 supplied by Haslewood 'should be secured out of the surplus pew rents of the church which should remain after payment thereout of £600 per annum which was to be applied in the payment of the expenses of keeping the church in repair and insured against fire, and the balance of £600 to the Minister of the church for the time being by way of stipend.'

So Haslewood contributed £4,000 towards the church of which he was to become incumbent. It seemed clear that the money was a loan and not a gift, but unfortunately this was not made clear to the parishioners of St. Mark's who were soon to take great exception to the manner of Haslewood's loan.

It might seem that Haslewood's central role in the financing of the church was the gesture of a wealthy man – and the fact that his address was New Bond Street, Mayfair, might affirm this view. This was not the case. Haslewood had, in fact, borrowed most of the £4,000 and, having borrowed it, eventually he would have to pay it back. The main method of repayment was through the pew rents. It was an accepted practice in the nineteenth century that better off parishioners could rent their pews and thus have them permanently reserved. Unfortunately the pew rents were never sufficient to pay back the loans and Haslewood was to run into great difficulty meeting the repayments. Still worse from the viewpoint of his standing in the parish was the fact that those who contributed to the other £4,000 had done so by donations and not by loans; they were led to believe Haslewood had *donated* the money – the

---

[1] Parish records, St. Mark's, Hamilton Terrace, 1847

fact he was paying himself back through the pew rents was not something he revealed till very much later. They were outraged that the pew rents should be used in this way and that his loan should become a permanent charge on the parish.

Ashby Haslewood was thus heavily in debt and like many desperate debtors he made things worse by trying to pay off his original debt with further loans. In 1852 he borrowed £778 from Mr. Charles Harrison to pay off his existing debts; by 1863 he was in debt to Harrison to the extent of £1,445 12s 6d. It was perhaps in financial desperation that Haslewood began speculating in railway shares – something which was brought to the attention of the Bishop of London and hardly helped in the attempt to create the right image for the founder of a new charity.

The year 1852 saw the first pupils enter St. John's Foundation School and the nadir of Haslewood's reputation – an unfortunate juxtaposition which made inevitable the committee's decision to sever their connection with him. In 1852 Haslewood attempted to promote a Bill in Parliament 'to vest the site and edifice of the Church of the District Parish of St. Mark's, St. Marylebone, in the Church Building Commissions, and for other purposes with relation to the said Church.' In seeking to promote this Bill, Haslewood revealed the real nature of his financing of the church, thus incurring widespread wrath and in seeking to gain a church rate – a tax – for St. Mark's, he provoked the fury of most of the parish. In Sir Benjamin Hall M.P., who came to the defence of his constituents, he found a new and highly-placed enemy.

The Bill proposed that £1,000 should be spent on the completion of the tower and spire of the church, the money 'to be retained on the credit of the surplus Pew Rents.' The Bill then proposed 'a clear annual stipend of £600 to the Incumbent'; a 5% interest rate for those who had advanced the original loan; the formation of a sinking fund for the payment of 'several foregoing principal sums' and the establishment of a church rate to be paid by the parishioners for the upkeep of the church. The objections to the Bill were many and it provoked massive opposition in the parish.

A petition was organised which stated that the parishioners had believed Haslewood had donated not lent the original sum and 'by expecting to obtain a regular income from the pew rents a fraud was practised upon the inhabitants of the district.' The petition finally raised objections to the church rate, complaining that it would be in addition to the rate already paid to the Parish of St. Marylebone. The petition stated: 'because the Church has been created by a voluntary association, and by means of voluntary subscriptions, the District at large ought not to be taxed for its support.'

Sir Benjamin Hall, the Liberal Member of Parliament for Marylebone, became involved in the dispute. Hall was a prominent political figure whose widely known views on the established church should have suggested to Haslewood a need to be cautious in his dealings with him. In 1834 he had been the seconder of a bill in the Commons, the aim of which was to abolish church rates; in a pamphlet published in 1850, 'A Letter to His Grace the Archbishop of Canterbury on the State of the Church', he had raised the issue of the abuse of the management of ecclesiastical property. In 1852 he had stated, 'Grants of public money must be confined to secular purposes.' Hall was bound to be hostile to Haslewood's scheme and he was a man of high influence – soon to be appointed President of the Board of Trade. He was, incidentally, the politician who agreed the construction of the bells in the tower of the parliament buildings at Westminster – Sir Benjamin Hall was 'Big Ben'. Unfortunately in his dealings with his M.P. Haslewood threw caution to the wind. The dispute began mildly enough – with Hall simply writing to enquire whether Haslewood intended to push ahead with the proposed Bill in view of the widespread hostility to it. Haslewood took this as inflammatory for he replied by saying he would make no comment 'until Sir Benjamin Hall has publicly withdrawn his injurious imputations.'

Hall, far from withdrawing, replied with a scathing and detailed indictment of Haslewood. In addition to the points made in the petition, Hall claimed Haslewood sought to increase his stipend to £600 *net* rather than £600 minus the provisions laid down by the trustees in 1847. This was a reference to the fact that the original terms of remuneration to the incumbent involved his receiving what was left of £600 per annum once the expenses of the church had been met. Hall concluded his letter with a flourish; 'every exertion will be used both by parishioners and their parliamentary representatives to expose and frustrate a scheme which is as unjust as it is discreditable to those who promote it.'

Whatever merits the proposed Bill might have had there can be no disputing that some of its provisions were aimed at securing and strengthening Haslewood's income and creating for him a regular revenue from church funds far outlasting his incumbency. It is not difficult, then, to see why, at the mildest, many were extremely wary of any venture associated with Haslewood's name. Nor were any dubious financial practices compensated for by an ability to promote and advertise his cause. In the field of public relations Haslewood obviously had little skill.

An innocent victim of this furore was Anthony Thomson, Haslewood's long-suffering curate and the first Headmaster of the School. Many believed that one reason Haslewood had founded the School was to ensure that the curate's stipend be paid by the School and not by himself. The responsibility for payment of a curate's stipend lay with the parish priest – before the School was established it was a further burden on Haslewood's very stretched resources. A neat solution would be to establish a school, make the curate the Headmaster and ensure he was paid from school funds. This is certainly what happened and thus the founding of St. John's School was seen by many as another of Ashby Haslewood's projects founded for a 'sordid motive.'

If an unflattering picture of Ashby Haslewood is emerging, then it is important to stress there were heroes in the story of the school's early years. Two of these heroes, Charles Churchill and Gordon Clark, were long-serving members of the Council who were to leave their considerable mark on the School. Anthony Thomson too lives on and is feted as the first Headmaster of the School – a portrait of him hangs in the main corridor alongside those who succeeded him. It was Charles Churchill, prosperous man of business and St. Mark's parishioner, who took it upon himself to distance the School from its founder by arranging the move of the School from Hamilton Terrace to Greville Mount: a distance of a mere five hundred metres but sufficient to break the link with Ashby Haslewood.

A further hero, little heralded, was the first secretary of the charity, W.B. Faulkner. He had the task of supervising the donations to the

School and overseeing the process of selection. (In brief, those who donated money to the School had the opportunity to elect pupils each year: a vote was granted for every five guineas donated.) This time-consuming duty was undertaken by Faulkner on top of his own parochial responsibilities; he was vicar of Hampstead. His work was made more burdensome by the obvious antipathy between himself and Ashby Haslewood. It is hard to understand why there was such dislike. Faulkner was an ardent supporter of the School; he performed his duties free of charge and frequently travelled considerable distances preaching about the School and its purpose. In the heated disputes he had with Ashby Haslewood it was clear whose side the committee took.

In June 1852 the committee recorded in their minutes their complete support for Faulkner in his arguments with Haslewood and later recorded regret at Haslewood's persistent hounding of the man. Faulkner himself wrote in exasperation to Haslewood after their final and most violent argument: 'This is not the first time you have attempted to draw me into a personal quarrel with yourself because it has been my painful, but necessary, duty in my position as secretary, to forward disagreeable communications to you. But I must take leave to remind you that all that has been unpleasant to you has been caused by your own want of straightforwardness and sincerity.'

Haslewood's deficiencies in character need not in themselves have hindered too seriously the development of the School. Founders of schools were not always bastions of moral and social excellence. Thomas Stevens, the founder of Bradfield, was interfering and inept and also had a financial motive for the founding of the school, a financial motive hidden beneath verbiage about Christian education and the need to provide for sons of the clergy. His financial irresponsibility was such that for long periods Bradfield masters received no pay. The inspiration behind Malvern's foundation was a Lea & Perrin's branch manager, Walter Burrow, whose social lowliness resulted in his never becoming a member of the Council. 'And when Burrow died in 1913 his part in the history of the College seems to have been so completely forgotten that

---

[1] R Blumenau, 'History of Malvern College'.

the school was not even represented at his funeral.'[1] One of the founders of Rossall was a Corsican hotelier and entrepreneur with little in the way of social or academic standing.

The difficulties with the founder were largely alleviated by the move to Greville Mount House, Kilburn. Ashby Haslewood continued to serve as priest at St. Mark's till 1864 when he became, briefly, Vicar of St. Michael's, Coventry, then Holy Trinity, Maidstone, before, in 1866, settling down for his final years as a parish priest at Mavesyn Ridware, Staffordshire. A flawed, foolish and possibly dishonest man, yet there has to be some sympathy for him. As he sank into comparative obscurity his school began to flourish. When he died it was firmly established at Leatherhead and was taking shape as a Victorian public school of some note.

CHAPTER THREE

A Moveable School
1854–1872

THE MOVE TO GREVILLE MOUNT AT KILBURN IN 1854 resolved the difficulties with Ashby Blair Haslewood, although – promoting himself as the rejected and scorned founder of the developing school – he continued to complain bitterly about how his project had been requisitioned by others. It would be pleasing to write that at last the School, after these teething problems, developed and prospered in the substantial house on Greville Mount which was rented by the committee. In its edition of May 9 1857 'The Illustrated London News' printed a woodcut of the School with the caption: 'This edifice presents a striking object to the traveller by the North and North West Railway, it being situated on the right of the line, on the London side of Kilburn Station'. The fact that 'The Illustrated London News' should devote such space to St. John's in 1857 would indicate that the School had made considerable progress during the five years of its existence and its three years at Kilburn. In an early concession to the demands of publicity and advertising, the committee erected a large sign across the top floor of the school house – 'St. John's Foundation School'- easily noticeable to the train passengers travelling in and out of the capital. St. John's, then, had begun to make an impact.

Greville Mount House, Greville Mount, Kilburn was a large, tall and imposing building whose appearance did suggest a now flourishing if still small charitable venture. By 1857 the numbers had risen from eight to thirty – all in receipt of a free education with free board and lodging. Funds and applicants were rising. Anthony Thomson was now the full-time Headmaster having severed all his links with St. Mark's, Hamilton Terrace. It would appear he was the only full-time member of staff at the time, being supported by several part-time assistants during the day. As well as overseeing their academic development Thomson cared for the children at evenings and weekends, where he was supported in these duties by a small domestic staff.

Anyone in search of Greville Mount House today will be disappointed. While St. Mark's continues to administer to its parishioners in the wide avenue of the elegant and prosperous Hamilton Terrace, Greville Mount House long ago gave way to a complex of modern flats. Greville Mount still exists, just off Greville Road, but only the liveliest imagination could conjure up a Victorian school from the scene which greets the modern traveller. What is noticeable is the extraordinary proximity of the School's two locations – a gentle five minute stroll is all that separates Greville Mount House from St. Mark's, Hamilton Terrace.

While 1857 saw the first piece of major national publicity for the School in 'The Illustrated London News', it also saw its second major crisis. This arose from the obvious financial difficulties being faced by the Headmaster and concluded with the pupils of the School being quickly transported away to an already established tutorial establishment in Walthamstow – their third location in three years. The financial problems of Anthony Thomson appear to have come about through a combination of stringency on the part of the council and a lack of financial acumen from the Headmaster. When Anthony Thomson had first been appointed headmaster – by Ashby Haslewood – he received £50 per annum per boy. But from this sum the funding of all aspects of a boy's upkeep had to be met – food, heating and the like. When the School moved to Kilburn and Thomson became full-time Headmaster his remuneration decreased – to £40 per annum per boy. Obviously there was some economic sense behind this – to maintain a per capita payment as the School went on expanding was not a viable proposition. Nevertheless it is clear that the Headmaster was soon facing difficulties. In 1854 he asked for an advance 'over and above his income' and then, in October 1857, he wrote to the committee requesting leave of absence 'in consequence of the state of my pecuniary affairs.' The request was refused. But Thomson took no heed and simply left the School, granting himself leave of absence. The committee had no option but to dismiss him. 'They have been compelled to bring to a close their connection with the Reverend A.F. Thomson and to remove their pupils from his care.'[1]

The wording here is interesting; the committee makes reference to 'their children'; they have handed over 'their children' to an outsider with whom they had struck a deal. The committee saw themselves at this stage as simply providing the wherewithal in order that the children would be fed, housed and educated by some other institution with whom they had made an arrangement.

There followed an anxious time for the committee; a school of thirty pupils was now without the Headmaster who was almost solely respon-sible for both their academic and pastoral well-being. An instant solution was required. The chairman of the committee, Charles Churchill, made contact with the Reverend Lewis Mercier whose father was a member of the School's committee and one of the School's examiners. Lewis Mercier had been the Headmaster of Edgbaston School but had just established his own school in Walthamstow. He was asked to take into his school the thirty foundationers abandoned by their former Headmaster. He agreed to do this, thus doubling the size of his school.

The move to Walthamstow was a desperate act of expedience. The committee, however, displayed considerable resourcefulness in putting a positive 'spin' on these events. The move to Walthamstow, they announced, 'obviates some of the objections which might be extended to a school strictly confined to the members of a particular class and profes-sion, and places the St. John's School more nearly in the position of one of the old established public schools of the country.'[2] It, of course, did no such thing. If anything it showed how *unlike* a public school St. John's was, given the fact that the absence of one individual nearly brought about the disintegration of the whole establishment.

[1] St. John's School Committee Minutes, 1857
[2] Anthony Thomson went on to live in France and became Chaplain at Dinard where he died in 1885; there is a memorial to him there in the church of St. Bartholomew.

So, at the end of 1857, the thirty pupils of St. John's Foundation School left Kilburn and travelled to Walthamstow. Greville Mount House was later to become a significant location in the history of another St. John's. The London College of Divinity moved into the house in 1863. It was later to become the theological college, St. John's College, Nottingham.

The brief two years at Walthamstow are the most mysterious of the School's history. Few personal recollections of pupils there have come to light. It is not even possible to be sure of the location of the school. The Reverend Lewis Page Mercier is recorded in the Walthamstow Archives as living in Grove Lane, Walthamstow – long since vanished – so it might be presumed that this was the address of the school. Lewis Mercier had only just ceased to be Headmaster of Edgbaston School and had just arrived from Birmingham to set up his own establishment. A graduate of University College, Oxford, he was thirty-seven years of age in 1857 and had been a Headmaster for eight years. His headmastership of St. John's was to be brief – four years – and it would appear he did not maintain the confidence of the committee. While he was placed in charge of the School during one of its most significant periods – the move to Clapton House in 1859 – he did not survive the important changes in the School's administration in 1861. In that year the committee extended their responsibilities and assumed control of every aspect of the School – both the raising of revenues for the charity and the education and pastoral well-being of the children. The first action of the new expanded committee was to sever their links with Lewis Mercier and, for the first time, advertise for an experienced career schoolmaster to be Headmaster.

The few recollections there are of Lewis Mercier indicate a round, jolly, loud and likeable man – something of a Dickensian character. The small school was dominated by his personality. All events at Walthamstow seemed to have occurred in a single room and boys recalled their minds being distracted from their studies each noon when the maids came into the schoolroom to prepare the lunch table and appetising smells wafted through from the kitchen.

Lewis Mercier's connection with St. John's is confused. No portrait of him hangs in the gallery of past Headmasters in the main corridor yet he is listed as the first Headmaster on the Dining Hall board – where there is no mention of poor Anthony Thomson, widely regarded as the School's first Head. In a sense he was not the Headmaster of St. John's for the boys were simply attached to his existing school – although he did make the move with them to Clapton House in 1859. While one might feel sympathy for Lewis Mercier, who seemingly strode to the rescue of the School in the 1857 crisis only to be discarded in 1861, there is in fact little need. Mercier was to find a profitable second career as a translator. In particular, he was to find some fame – and indeed a little notoriety – as the leading translator into English of the works of the popular French novelist, Jules Verne. His translations were to become the most widely read and influential of all those of Jules Verne's novels. Unfortunately, Lewis Mercier had a tendency to reduce the original text and to offer rather mechanical translations. Today he is vilified by Jules Verne scholars who see him – and his supposedly inadequate translations – as one reason why the author does not receive the academic acclaim due to him. An American scholar, Walter Miller, writing of Mercier's 'deliberate censorship' of 'Twenty Thousand Leagues Under the Sea' wrote: 'these cuts, often subtracting thirty to forty percent of Verne's text . . . naturally weaken his story line, characterisations, humour and the integrity of his ideas.' It seems Lewis Mercier might have taken exception to some of Verne's political and religious ideas and simply removed them from the text; in addition, when he came across sections of manuscript difficult to translate, he left them out. But the translations remained hugely influential and were 'still the main source for revised translations' as late as the 1960s. Lewis Mercier produced his translations while working as the Chaplain to the Foundling Hospital. He was still performing these two tasks when he died in 1875 at the age of fifty-five.

In 1859 the School moved to Clapton House – the third move in five years. Those eight-year-old boys who had walked through the door of Anthony Thomson's home in Hamilton Terrace in January 1852 would complete their eight years of free education at Clapton House and would have spent their schooldays in four different locations. This rootless and insecure image was not one the School sought to promote but was brought about through a number of unfortunate events. It was remarkable that the School had survived these early tribulations – many schools founded at the same time as St. John's did not. Three actions taken by the committee between 1859 and 1861 displayed a determination to survive and prosper. First, in 1859 the move to the large and spacious Clapton House; second the extension of the committee's responsibilities and, third, the appointment of a new Headmaster.

Clapton House was a large and prestigious building set in nine acres of parkland. The property was owned by the Reverend Thomas Baden Powell whose family held the livings of both St. James, Clapton and Newick, near Uckfield in Sussex. The building had housed a school prior to the arrival of St. John's – a proprietary school called Clapton House School. Thomas Baden Powell, who was an uncle of Robert Baden Powell, was a great supporter of the school and a regular contributor to the charity. He was only too pleased to rent the property to the committee and so in 1859 60 pupils – 35 of them the Foundationers of St. John's and 25 the private pupils of Lewis Mercier – began a new school life at Clapton House.

The boys would have noticed – if not appreciated – their changed circumstances. Clapton House was a very grand and spacious house located at the centre of considerable educational activity largely instigated by dynamic and energetic clergymen. At the time of the School's move to Clapton, the Rector of neighbouring Hackney was responsible for a Charity School, a Grammar School, two proprietary schools, a 'school of industry', an infant school and an 'orphan asylum.' The 'orphan asylum', incidentally, which was a close neighbour to Clapton House, was to become Reed's School, Cobham. The new location of St. John's probably explains why in 1860, after less than a year at Clapton, the School became one of the beneficiaries of the enormous charitable giving of the generous and extremely wealthy Angela Burdett Coutts. Miss (later Baroness) Burdett Coutts gave an annual donation to the School of at least £500. While she was a committed Anglican and gave extensively to church charities, she only began giving to St. John's when the School moved to Clapton; it would appear that it was the location of the School rather than the nature of the charity which attracted Burdett Coutts' money.

'Clapton House must have been a unique establishment. It had a huge marble entrance hall, a ballroom and very superior baths. In the grounds were wide gravel walks with a double row of stately and umbrageous elms.' Thus wrote W.R. Power in his history of Hackney Downs Schools. The boys of St. John's, then, were at last being housed in grand and spacious premises.

At this key moment in the School's history the committee advertised for a new Headmaster and in 1861 they appointed to the post Edwards Hawkins. He was Head of Classics at Brighton College which at the time was a breeding ground for public school headmasters. Even though it had been established just six years before St. John's, Brighton College had quickly gained a reputation. Of Hawkins' staff-room colleagues eight became headmasters: Frederick Walker at Manchester Grammar School and later St. Paul's; Henry Day and Frederick Hepenstall who succeeded each other at Sedbergh and William Grignon who became Headmaster of Felsted. Edwards Hawkins' appointment is a key moment in the development of the School – the committee now felt confident enough to go in search of a good Headmaster and Edwards Hawkins must have felt the move to the School represented a positive career opportunity for him – indicating a new status for the School.

So for the moment the period of movement, insecurity and anxiety seemed to be over. At the beginning of the 1860s the School had survived early storms and now seemed set to embark upon a period of expansion. The three locations in five years had prevented any opportunity for establishing a regional identity and for developing the loyalty and services that would lead on from this. The movement from one rented property to another meant there could be no building programme, no opportunity to design a facility to suit the needs of the School, and no opportunity for proper recreational facilities. At Clapton House things might change. There remained, though, a difficulty. Clapton House – like the other St. John's properties – was rented. The period of progress and expansion the School now embarked upon would inevitably create new pressures on space. Within four years of moving to Clapton House the committee were pleading with Thomas Baden Powell to sell the property to them so they could embark upon a building programme. Keen supporter of the School though he was, the owner of the property had no intention of selling. By the middle of the 1860s it had become obvious that the School might have to move once more.

CHAPTER FOUR

The Move to Leatherhead

THE REVEREND EDWARDS COMERFORD HAWKINS BECAME Headmaster of St. John's School at Clapton in August 1861. In his early thirties, he was the son of a Hertfordshire doctor and had been educated at Marlborough – one of its very early pupils – and Exeter College, Oxford.

A talented and ambitious schoolmaster keen to advance his career, he must have seen St. John's as a wise career move – and as has been said – this indicates much about the School's new status. Nevertheless the School remained small in scale and ambitions; there were sixty pupils aged between eight and sixteen. With its size and age limit it could not seriously offer itself as a major academic institution. It remained essentially a charity school whose main purpose was to provide a *free* education rather than a *good* education. There was no chance of entry to university and there was little opportunity to play competitive games – increasingly seen as a measure of status in the world of the public school. In the early 1860s St. John's was still far from being a public school though it became quite clear that Edwards Hawkins' aim was to turn it into one. Very quickly, though, it became apparent that if St. John's was to expand and take on the characteristics of more prestigious establishments even the stylish Clapton House – such an advance on previous locations – would not be of sufficient size: a problem compounded by the fact that the School did not own the property so there was little possibility of building around the site.

An additional factor in early concerns about Clapton House was the appearance of Mr. Fearon from the Schools Inquiry Commission. In 1864 this Commission had been established, under the chairmanship of Lord Taunton, to investigate those secondary schools which were not the 'public schools' investigated in the earlier Clarendon Commission. There was widespread concern about the provision of secondary education – and indeed elementary education – throughout the country and the government was keen to establish some sort of uniform pattern. The School's committee, however, did not welcome this governmental interference. Charles Churchill wrote to the commissioner arguing that St. John's could be of no interest to the commission because it had no endowments, charged no fees and was entirely dependent on voluntary contributions. The ploy did not work and the commissioner did visit the School and did look into its teaching and administrative arrangements. In fact the report was satisfactory – with only a negative reference to some of the classroom and dayroom accommodation – unlike that for Christ's Hospital which, as a consequence of the Taunton Report, had to make large-scale changes to all aspects of the School's organisation.

In 1864 Edwards Hawkins faced the problem of where the French Master could conduct his classes: he decided on the Dining Hall 'at any time when not required for meals.' In the summer of 1864, the committee promised a sum 'not exceeding three hundred pounds' to be used to convert a playroom into a schoolroom. But the committee were constantly restricted in what they could do in terms of extensions and improvements because they did not own the freehold of Clapton House. As early as 1864 the committee expressed an interest in purchasing the freehold to enable them to extend the school premises. The Reverend Thomas Baden Powell, failed to respond to letters on the subject with the consequence that on 1 April 1865 the Treasurers, Gordon Clark and George Brooking, visited him at Newick, his country house in Sussex. The visit at least provoked a response, for Powell shortly afterwards did write to the committee but only to affirm that 'he adhered to his purpose of not parting with the Freehold of the Clapton House estate.'

With that option removed from further consideration, a committee member who was an architect, Joseph Good, was asked to give an opinion 'on the feasibility and propriety of additional buildings, for dormitories and Dining Hall, under a present lease or under a strengthened lease.' The committee were obviously pessimistic about the outcome of Good's enquiries for, at the same meeting, the Secretary was asked 'to enquire about an eligible tract of land, or about ten acres, suitable for building a new school premises upon.'

So as early as May 1865 enquiries were being made into the possibility of new premises. But these enquiries arose only because of the difficulties involved in attempting to undertake changes at Clapton. Far from there being a desire to leave London for a spacious rural setting, the motive for most moves from the city by other schools, there was a real reluctance to depart from Clapton; so much so that in December 1865 a further attempt was made to deal with Powell. A sub-committee was formed 'to gain information about property in the neighbourhood of London and to see how we stand with the Reverend T.B. Powell as regards Clapton House.'

It was not until December 1866, faced with Powell's continued refusal either to sell or extend the Clapton House lease, that the committee at last determined to find new premises. Factors behind the reluctance to leave Clapton must have been the realisation of the costs involved in constructing new premises, the difficulty of finding an area with convenient communication links to the many areas from which the School drew its pupils as well as fatigue at the thought of yet another move. Nevertheless, once it was obvious there was no alternative but to move if more sons of clergy were to enter the School, the committee acted swiftly. In March 1867 a 16 acre property at Walton-on-Thames was considered, but this proved too expensive and was sold subsequently for £11,900. In response to this setback the sub-committee were asked 'to consider and report on the desirability of taking the second house at Clapton adjoining the Clapton House in case of its becoming vacant.' Still, then, there was a reluctance to leave Clapton – three years after the rejection of the original approach to Powell. In the view of the sub-committee the second house at Clapton was unsuitable, so they returned to their search for other premises. In June 1867 sites at St. George's Hill,

Weybridge, and Reigate were considered but, before serious thought was given to these, a plot of land at Leatherhead was brought to the attention of the committee. On 12 August a special meeting was convened 'to consider the propensity of purchasing twelve acres of land at Leatherhead at a cost of £2,500.' The subject was discussed 'in connection with other offers of land which had been presented to the Building Committee' but the Leatherhead plot, and price, seemed to fit requirements. It was agreed that the treasurers should be asked immediately to put down a deposit on the land and four days later, on 16 August, Gordon Clark, one of the two treasurers, wrote that 'he had signed a contract on behalf of the Trustees and that a Deposit of 10 per cent – £250 – had been paid.'

Leatherhead was a small but rapidly expanding community 20 miles south of London and equidistant between the important centres of Epsom and Dorking. Its population had nearly tripled between 1841 and 1891, with the most rapid expansion taking place after 1871; a population of 1,700 in 1841 became 2,500 in 1871 and 4,500 in 1901. This population expansion was largely due to the development of a railway link to London during the 1860s. By 1871 Leatherhead was well served by railways with two railway companies, the London – Brighton – South Coast and the London – South West having stations in the town. Leatherhead would have been only slightly less convenient than London for boys travelling considerable distances.

The move to Leatherhead would turn out to be a most fortunate moment in the history of the School, its arrival happily coinciding with the transformation of a small village into a major London commuter centre. In the 1860s and 1870s Leatherhead was throwing away its agricultural past – old family jobs were being replaced with work in brewing, coachbuilding, tanning, shoe-making and building; and then came the London commuter. In later years some traditionalists were to express frustration at the task of running a boarding school in the suburbs, but the location of Leatherhead, with its prosperous inhabitants giving access to a huge day pupil market, was to serve the School well when educational fashions changed.

With the deposit on the site paid the committee now faced two more formidable problems: firstly, of course, the full purchase price had to be paid and, secondly, and far more serious, funds needed to be raised to construct a building on the site. Gordon Clark suggested the trustees be approached to release funds for the payment of the land since they controlled over £10,000 in investments. The committee then intended to set up a special Building Fund and seek donors for this. The trustees, of course, were not free to dispose of funds as they wished but could do so only in accordance with the principles of the Charity. Where money had been specifically donated or subscribed to fund board, lodging and tutorial fees for sons of the clergy, it would be difficult to channel such funds into other projects.

In September 1867, with the committee facing this new, enormous, self-imposed financial burden, a letter was received from one of the three trustees, William Phelps, a partner of Phelps and Bennett, solicitors:

'I have much pleasure in informing you that on mentioning to a liberal friend and client the contract which the committee of St. John's Foundation School have entered into for the purchase of a site for a new School House he has directed me to acquaint the Committee that he will make a present of the site to them. I will arrange to hand you a cheque for £2,500 whenever the Committee may require the money to complete the purchase.'

The donor was anonymous; the receipt given to Phelps stated: 'Received of a friend of the School.' It was later revealed that the donor was Henry Dawes of 6, Hyde Park Gardens. When Dawes died his family was asked if a member would like to serve on the committee, but the offer was declined.

Henry Dawes' generous gift meant the purchase of the land could go ahead. In December 1867 negotiations commenced with the owner of the land, the Reverend John Byron of Elmsore Hardwicke in Gloucestershire, and these were not finalised till June 1868. Meanwhile a building sub-committee was set up 'for the purpose of arranging the new School House at Leatherhead.' A prominent member of the sub-committee was the indefatigable James Hessey, Headmaster of Merchant Taylors'. Hessey had been a member of the earlier sub-committee which had examined the feasibility of a move and he was, at the same time, dealing with the Headmaster over the latter's worries about the quality of the intake into the School. Hessey, an invaluable link between

Headmaster and committee, communicated with Edwards Hawkins to ensure the new building met the requirements of the teaching staff as well as the requirements of the committee. In January 1868 Edwards Hawkins was requested to draw up 'a statement of the accommodation necessary for 100 boys.' He was also asked to examine facilities at the Clergy Orphan School and at King's School, Canterbury. It is difficult to see why the latter school was chosen for comparative purposes – it was probably geographical convenience, for the Clergy Orphan School was also based in Canterbury and the Headmaster could easily look around King's School while in the area. There were obvious similarities between St. John's and the Clergy Orphan School – apart from serving similar needs both schools had been situated at St. John's Wood. An act of munificence similar to Henry Dawes' had enabled the Clergy Orphan School to establish itself in Canterbury in 1855.

In January 1868 the committee appointed two architects, Messrs. Good and Ferrey, to design the school building. With the land purchased and architects appointed there was then a hiatus, caused by the realisation of the extent of the financial commitment undertaken. The architects produced an estimate for the building of £13,915. This obviously caused the committee considerable dismay for the sums coming into the Building Fund would not meet anything like this amount. In March 1869 £3,000 was transferred from the Reserve Fund, controlled by the trustees, to the Building Fund. The committee pessimistically agreed in that same month that there was no possibility of commencing the building programme in 1869. The architects were also asked to 'reconsider the plans in order to determine whether any or what part of the building can be omitted at the outset seeing that the Committee are not likely to raise at once funds sufficient to meet the whole expense.' They were also asked to 'consider whether any suggestions may be made with a view to greater economy.'

The situation was no less bleak at the start of 1870. A reduction of £1,500 was achieved through economies in the use of materials and the withdrawal of plans for a lodge, for stables and an additional bedroom in the Headmaster's house. But £12,415 still seemed a difficult sum to raise and in March 1870 a motion was put before the committee that no building contract be entered into 'until the committee are in a better financial position.' This motion, though, was defeated and it was agreed instead that: 'Tenders be obtained for the entire building according to the Plans and Specifications which have been approved and that it be a stipulation with the contractor to make one estimate for the carcase of the Building and another for carrying out the remainder of the specification, giving the committee the power to reconsider the second contract.' In April 1870, Messrs. Goddard and Son of Farnham, who provided the cheapest tender, were appointed on the conditions as laid down in March. They quoted £12,490 for the whole building; £8,757 for the 'carcase' and £3,733 for the joining and engineering. On 16 May 1870, consent was given for the building to commence; the contractor was to be paid in instalments – the first (£1,500) due the following September.

The committee, then, had come through a period of considerable misgivings about the venture upon which they had embarked. The practical task that had been set was daunting and made no easier by the fact that all the time, while finding funds for the Leatherhead project, Clapton House had to be maintained.

The committee were unaware of the other major obstacle to fund-raising at this time. In 1859, at the time of the move to Clapton House, the committee decided to appoint a full-time administrator. The School had relied on the hard work of part-timers in its first eight years of existence but the work now involved meant a full-time professional was needed. The first administrator of St. John's was Robert Newman and his appointment could not have been more unfortunate. Very quickly Newman began to embezzle the funds of the School. When he came to St. John's he had exemplary credentials, having been the secretary of St. Mary's Hospital, Paddington. But his career at the School was a dishonest saga of deceit.

The extent of Newman's embezzlement seriously undermined the work of the committee. When his crime was discovered, by his office clerk, a committee of enquiry was set up which calculated that Newman had been helping himself to sums of money since 1862. The total amount he embezzled was calculated at £3,856 3s. 9d. which had been amassed over an eleven-year period. To give some idea of the significance of this amount: in 1873 the total sum raised through donations and subscriptions was £4,504; in 1862 it had been £2,417 5s. 6d.; the salary of the Headmaster in 1865 was £322 per annum, and Newman's own salary was £250 per annum. It was particularly distressing that a large part of the embezzlement occurred at just the time when the School was desperate to raise money for the Leatherhead move.

There was a debate over what to do about Newman. Dr. Hessey, prominent committee member, feared a criminal prosecution would lead to bad publicity; it would 'greatly damage the character of our administration and shake confidence in our society.' A civil action, however, was brought against Newman and 'judgement obtained and enforced against his effects.' But the total amount repaid by Newman appears to have been only £595 10s.7d. Through his fraud, the School had lost well over £3,000 in an eleven-year period and Newman's embezzlement amounted to an annual sum which was more than his annual salary.

Newman must have been a particularly thick-skinned rogue. After his dismissal, and the civil action against him, he wrote to the chairman of the committee asking if he, the chairman, might agree to act as a referee for him in his search for future employment. The chairman's reply can be imagined.

Despite this setback the building project did get under way. It lasted from 1870 to 1872 and was overseen by a sub-committee in which, again, Dr. Hessey played an important role.

This sub-committee had a wider brief, though, than just the supervision of the building – it also considered the terms of employment of Headmaster and staff once the move to Leatherhead was completed. The move, then, was not just the provision of a new location but an opportunity to put right some of the administrative and pastoral problems that had occurred in the past.

An extra week's holiday was granted to the boys in the summer break and the School was scheduled to open on 23 August 1872. The lease on Clapton House was to be surrendered at the end of September 1872 with agreement 'to quit at Lady Day 1873' (25 March). Unfortunately, though, an unexpected delay in proceedings occurred when in July 1872

Dixon Peach, the Second Master, died. A successor was quickly appointed, A.C. Pearson, but the School's opening had to be put back by a week. So on 30 August 1872, after delays, setbacks, doubts and tribulations, St. John's School opened in its new school house at Leatherhead. There it was to remain and prosper.

CHAPTER FIVE

The Teachers and the Taught

I T IS PERHAPS UNFAIR ON EDWARDS HAWKINS THAT HIS headmastership should be seen as a foundation stone for the extraordinary achievements of his successor, Arthur Rutty. Yet there has to be truth in this verdict. Edwards Hawkins very quickly identified the three key problems which faced St. John's if it hoped to become a 'public school' – the absence of both a coherent entry policy and a sixth form education and the single category of person whom the School served. He endeavoured to do something about these issues but had only limited success. What he did do was move the School to a freehold property with considerable acreage where expansion was possible and he did create a positive image for the School – factors which were to make the later work of Arthur Rutty that much easier.

It might be a convenient moment, before considering the School's huge advance at the end of the nineteenth century, to see if a picture can be constructed of both the pupils and the teachers during the School's early and formative years. This is no easy task. In 1886 'The Johnian' magazine appears – at last the voice of the pupil, albeit a rather sanitised and establishment voice; and as the turn of the century approaches we begin to hear and read the reminiscences of old boys and teachers. But the 1850s and 1860s can be conjured up only by speculating upon the few facts and glimpses we have. It is also, of course, unhelpful to offer generalisations about groups of very diverse people. To contemplate the characteristics of the 'typical Johnian' of the 1850s and 1860s is as unrealistic – and insulting – a task as considering the 'typical' pupil, teacher or governor at the start of the twenty-first century.

The eight pupils who comprise the first intake of the School in January 1852 are known (see the list on pages 101–2). Six of the eight pupils were voted into the School by those who contributed to the foundation – a single vote for every five guineas donated. Of the other two pupils, one was nominated by the churchwardens of St. Mark's, and the other was the personal nomination of the School's founder, Ashby Haslewood. This policy of allowing the church and its vicar to have nominations was abandoned when the School moved to Greville Mount – from 1854 all pupils were voted in at an election.

These first pupils seem to have come from sorry backgrounds. Robert Brocklebank was one of ten children and his family is described as 'suffering great distress'. Archibald Cole was one of nine children, two of whom were crippled. Details of the backgrounds of the children were compiled by the Secretary who then passed on the information to those entitled to a vote. As the School's reputation spread, it became necessary for an inspection team to be established to check on the validity of the background details of the boys. It was not unknown for a clergyman to exaggerate his woes in order to gain sympathy from the electors.

The boys travelled from all over England and Wales – an important factor when considering the location of the School; it had to be at the centre of a transport network. The areas from which most boys came in the 1850s and 1860s were the dioceses of Norwich, Salisbury and Exeter. Local boys, those whose fathers worked in the London diocese, were few: none at all in the 1850s and only a handful throughout most of the 1860s. The School never rose in size to more than 65 pupils until the move to Leatherhead. This smallness of scale, alongside the age limit of the pupils of eight to sixteen, precluded any serious involvement in competitive sport. No record of school teams exists before 1878, by which time there were one hundred pupils in the School. The early locations of the School – at Hamilton Terrace, Greville Mount and Walthamstow – were in congested, urban and heavily populated areas. The spacious grounds at Clapton House did offer opportunities for sport and the first rugby and cricket games were played on the spacious lawns there. Two other popular early sports played at the School were paper-chasing and fives – one of the first developments at Leatherhead was the construction of fives courts.

While competitive sports with other schools were rare in the early years, there seems to have been enthusiastic participation amongst the pupils. There are references to individual athletics competitions held in the early days at both Clapton and Leatherhead. A particularly gifted runner was Anthony Hope Hawkins, son of the Headmaster. One assistant master remarked that the other boys found it irritating watching young Anthony race in ahead of the field with his father joining him in the final few strides shouting 'Anthony wins! Anthony wins!'. It was perhaps wise that young Anthony was packed off to Marlborough, his father's old school, when he was thirteen.

Most – but certainly not all – early Johnians seem to have been reasonably well-disciplined young men. It is noticeable that soon after the School was established at Hamilton Terrace a local schoolmaster endeavoured to set up a preparatory school which, he claimed, would be 'in connection with St. John's Foundation School'. Nothing came of the project but it is interesting to note that the St. John's link was seen as a positive selling point. In the late 1850s, a 'national school' was opened in the St. Mark's parish – national schools were church-administered elementary schools. The parishioners were appalled by the rowdiness of the pupils and unfavourable comparisons were made with the earlier pupils of St. John's.

A very effective manner of keeping the pupils well-behaved was to threaten them with removal from the Foundation. It was stressed that they were in receipt of very generous charitable provision and if they stepped out of line there was always someone else awaiting a place at the School. This point was made with particular emphasis to the 'marginal' child – he who had just got into the School. A letter was sent to the parents by the chairman of the committee congratulating the child on receiving sufficient votes to be elected but pointing out that he had only just scraped in and his position, therefore, would be constantly under review.

Occasionally, however, serious punishment was required. In

December 1854 a boy named O'Connor got into very serious trouble – the nature of his misdemeanour, unfortunately, is not recorded. The committee requested the Headmaster to 'inflict a sound flogging with birch rod in the presence of the whole school and the committee and the boy be kept at school during the Christmas holiday and subjected to further punishment as the committee shall think fit.' The picture of a lonely O'Connor wandering the school building on Christmas Day awaiting a further thrashing on the whim of the Headmaster or the committee is a pathetic one. A frequent act of indiscipline at Clapton seems to have been the bolster fight. Boys would form up in groups on the spacious landings and engage in combat after lights out. If caught, however, the consequences were dire – a 'thrashing with a trunk strap' by the Second Master.

A factor which links the plight of boy and teacher was – and is – the examination. The first Johnians had an internal Annual Examination each summer. The reports of these examiners usually made encouraging reading. The Reverend Morgan Cowie, a Schools' Inspector and also a St. John's committee member, examined the boys in Mathematics in 1856 and 1857. 'The boys seem carefully trained,' he wrote, 'and a great deal of work is got out of them all, with very few exceptions.' In 1862 Charles Granville Clarke, Fellow of Worcester College, Oxford and a former colleague of Edwards Hawkins at Brighton College, examined the boys in the Humanities. He concluded: 'I am able to say that the papers in English, History and Scripture, and any of those in Grammar, were such as would have been expected from boys two or even three years older.' Dr. James Hessey, the influential Headmaster of Merchant Taylors, examined the boys in 1863. He wrote: 'The boys are beginners in Algebra and the questions are not hard; but they are remarkably well answered by some boys. One boy obtained 98 out of 100. The Arithmetic papers being the same as those set at Merchant Taylors I put these into the hands of Mr. Bowker, our examiner in Arithmetic. His account of the boys' proficiency is so satisfactory that I enclose his letter. Eleven boys attempted the French paper. Their exercises have different degrees of accuracy but there are two or three which show considerable care and thought.'

So these reports give an encouraging picture. Yet we know that the Headmaster was unhappy about the academic achievement of his school. When he provided a statement for the committee on the eve of the move to Leatherhead, he concentrated exclusively on the problems associated with a non-selective entry. This was something he had complained about since becoming Headmaster – and it was a theme to be pursued by his successor, Arthur Rutty. Boys arrived at St. John's, Edwards Hawkins wrote, 'whose abilities and moral tone were far below the level for deriving advantage from the education supplied by the school.' The Headmaster's particular concern was that, given a non-selective entry, many boys 'linger in the middle and below the middle of the school till the time of their departure at sixteen, to the serious damage of the intellectual standard and of the tone of the masses.' Academic progress depended on the achievement of standards – a boy could only move up to a higher class once a specified standard was reached. With a non-selective entry many boys were left stranded in the middle forms till they left.

The optimistic tone of the Annual Examination reports, then, needs to be matched against the frequent and consistent worries of the Headmaster. The Annual Examination was, by the fearsome standards of today, a cosy affair. Two or three gentlemen, all with strong links with the School or the Headmaster, spent a day at the School in mid-June. Each boy was examined both orally and in writing. Immediately after the examination prizes were awarded, and these were presented on Prize Day. There was no attempt to establish rigid criteria and comparisons with other schools were only based on the random observations of the inspectors. It is noticeable, too, that while favourable examination reports are quoted at length in the School's Annual Report, sometimes there is only a brief reference to the examination – just a simple expression of gratitude to the examiners for their time and effort; and after 1864 the examiners' reports are removed altogether from the Annual Report – a document, it must be remembered, published for donors and designed to portray as flattering a picture of the School as possible.

St. John's pursued a traditional curriculum with a heavy emphasis on the Classics. There was some broadening in 1866 when a series of lectures was introduced in electricity and chemistry. It was to be some while before science became an integral part of the curriculum – but the lectures arranged for the boys did indicate that the School was considerably more progressive than some. Similarly, there was interest in the quality of French teaching at the School – an early report did pick up inadequacies here but Edwards Hawkins was quick to act, employing a new teacher and arranging better classroom facilities. A limiting factor in the development of a broader curriculum was, of course, the training of the teaching staff, most of whom were classicists.

With the boys being required to leave at sixteen, there was obviously no sixth form provision. Edwards Hawkins appealed regularly to the committee to allow bright pupils to stay on to prepare for university entrance. He got nowhere. The view of the committee was that a boy staying on past sixteen was occupying the space needed for a boy entering the School at eight. So the best St. John's could offer its brightest pupils was a scholarship at an established public school. M.G. Lohr, one of ten children of a Norwich clergyman, won a scholarship to Wellington in 1867. Edmund Luce, from Faversham in Kent, won a scholarship to Oundle in 1870 (he went on to teach at Eton). In 1866 Edwards Hawkins tried desperately to hold on to the School's brightest pupil, William Grundy. When it became apparent that the committee would not permit Grundy to remain at St. John's, the Headmaster made arrangements whereby Grundy would lodge with the Headmaster at Leatherhead while receiving tuition at Charterhouse. But the committee firmly rejected all the Headmaster's pleas, stating firmly that the charity did not provide board and lodging for a pupil to be educated elsewhere. (The committee were similarly unsympathetic towards the several wealthy benefactors prepared to offer scholarships for St. John's pupils if they went to Oxford, Cambridge or provincial universities). William Grundy's problem was resolved when he won the Osborne Scholarship to Rossall. He went on to achieve a first class honours degree at Worcester College, Oxford and became Headmaster of Malvern. He died aged 41 in 1891 having collapsed while playing rackets with the boys.

While the teachers became frustrated at losing their most able pupils, the committee took considerable pride in the achievement of scholarships to other schools: all those who left for established public schools received glowing testimonials in the Annual Report. This clearly shows the growing dichotomy between staff and committee – the former wanting the opportunity to teach sixth form pupils and the latter seeking to remain loyal to the principles of the charity.

The greatest academic achievement, then, for a Johnian was to obtain a scholarship to a leading public school. Only a handful of bright boys were able to move on in this way. Most boys left at sixteen with no qualifications other than the internal assessment conducted through the Annual Examination.

But Edwards Hawkins was keen for able boys to sit external examinations. These had been growing in significance since the late 1850s. Again, though, the Headmaster came up against the hostility of the committee who were reluctant to pay examination entry fees. Two boys were entered for the 'Cambridge Non-Gremial Examinations' in 1859 and both were awarded '2nd class in honours'. In 1860 one boy sat for the 'Oxford Middle-Class Examination' and was '3rd in order of merit in 1st class of honours'. But when the Headmaster tried to enter a group of boys for the Oxford and Cambridge Local Examinations in 1865 the committee refused to pay the examination fees and the boys were not entered. The Headmaster, though, eventually won this battle and by the late 1860s many boys were sitting external examinations.

The attitude of the committee towards the educational advancement of the pupils does seem to have prompted frustration from the teaching staff, which doubled from five to ten between the mid-1860s and mid-1870s. There was rapid staff turn-over in the mid-1860s which did cause concern and in 1866 a sub-committee was appointed 'to see Mr. Hawkins and the other masters with a view of ascertaining the duties of the several masters and obtaining information to guide the committee in the selection of new undermasters and in making future arrangements.'

Several factors seemed to have been behind the dissatisfaction – certainly the seeming lack of interest from the committee in raising the academic profile of the School, but also the Headmaster's terms of employment. When Edwards Hawkins was appointed in 1861 he struck a deal with the committee whereby he could bring into the School up to six private boarding pupils of his own. He agreed to pay the committee £50 per annum per boy and then could charge whatever fee he wished to the parents. The assistant teachers at the School resented this arrangement and it was withdrawn in 1865 – to be replaced two years later by an arrangement involving just day boys. The removal of the Headmaster's boarders did solve one cause of resentment – the fact that assistant masters had to care for these pupils at evenings and weekends but all remuneration went to the Headmaster. The Headmaster could now bring into the School up to ten day boys 'to be educated as pupils of the Headmaster'. He paid £7 per annum to the committee whilst charging £20 per annum to the parents. This arrangement took his income close to £350 per annum – three times more than the most senior of the assistant teachers. Further cause of staff discontent was the inability of the School to offer promotion. There were no houses and thus no house-masterships. Housemasterships at the end of the nineteenth century were crucial positions carrying status, a qualification for career advancement and the potential for additional income. At St. John's the opportunity for additional income was the monopoly of the Headmaster.

Yet the plight of the Johnian teacher could not have been too unhappy for several former pupils of the School were keen to return once they had graduated. Arthur Walpole left the School in 1867, and returned to teach in 1882. He later taught at Rossall. William Ragg left the School in 1879 and returned in 1884; he became Headmaster of Hereford Cathedral School in 1897. (His brother Robert Ragg, also at St. John's, became Headmaster of Reigate Grammar School in 1899). William Beaumont left the School in 1879 and returned as a master in 1887. He taught for twenty years at St. John's before becoming Headmaster of St. Michael's, Tenbury. The most committed of all Johnians, though, must be Arthur Fraser Smith; he left the School in 1876, studied Classics at London University and returned to St. John's in 1885 where he continued to teach until 1932! Arthur Fraser Smith's 47 year teaching career at St. John's is beaten by Henry Hagreen, the Art teacher, who taught at the School from 1858 to 1908. But the longest serving St. John's employee was Mr. Gray who worked in the school office from 1911 to 1969.

This body of Johnians, it must be remembered, had had to leave St.

John's at sixteen to prepare for university entrance elsewhere. Yet they returned to St. John's to teach and were part of that group of teachers who assisted the pioneering Headmaster, Arthur Rutty, as he transformed St. John's into a public school.

CHAPTER SIX

Arthur Rutty and the Making of a Public School
(1883–1909)

EDWARDS HAWKINS RESIGNED HIS HEADMASTERSHIP IN 1883 to become vicar of St. Bride's, Fleet Street (where he remained until his death in 1906). He was in his middle fifties and had directed the affairs of the School for over twenty years. When he became Headmaster there were 49 pupils in the School and when he left there were 140. While managing the expansion in numbers he had also supervised the move to Leatherhead. His leadership was undoubtedly one of considerable achievement. Yet in 1883 St. John's remained essentially a charity school with no sixth form, no process of selection and little involvement within a network of other schools.

A part of Edwards Hawkins would have been happy with the move into the heart of London. He had achieved all he could for the School and it was time to make way for a younger man. He had strong literary and political interests. He was a friend of George Meredith, the novelist, and had visited him frequently at his home at Flint Cottage, Box Hill. He was active in Liberal politics. Fleet Street would be an exhilarating change from Leatherhead. Yet he always had the fondest regard for the School and its location and chose to be buried in Leatherhead Parish Church. (Edwards Hawkins had strong literary connections; his nephew was Kenneth Grahame, author of 'The Wind in the Willows'; his grandson was the historian, Keith Feiling; his son, of course, was Sir Anthony Hope, author of 'The Prisoner of Zenda', knighted at the end of the Great War for services to the wartime government. Anthony Hope was also buried in Leatherhead Parish Church).

Edwards Hawkins' successor was Arthur Rutty. Under his headmastership the School was transformed into a public school. Arthur Rutty became a member of the Headmasters' Conference (HMC) in 1890; St. John's was listed in the Public Schools' Yearbook from 1892; the school's brightest pupils gained scholarships at Oxford and Cambridge; its sporting teams competed successfully with some of the most famous schools in the country; its expanding roll comprised a mixture of those with free places, those with subsidised places and those paying competitive fees. To cope with the increased numbers a large building programme was undertaken. Within the School, houses were created to give boys a focus for their involvement and to provide promotion to housemasterships for ambitious schoolmasters. The St. John's that we recognise at the beginning of the twenty-first century was the work of Arthur Rutty.

There were, of course, factors which assisted the new Headmaster. Edwards Hawkins had put in the minds of committee members the need to think about the quality of the educational provision; advantages did accrue from property ownership; the expanding teaching staff was ambitious; the strong clergy connection meant there was influence that could be exploited at Oxford and Cambridge. But there can be no question that the School was fortunate in its choice of new Headmaster.

Arthur Foster Rutty was born in the City of London in 1846. His father was a shipbroker. He won a scholarship to Merchant Taylors in 1856 and a further scholarship took him to Pembroke College, Cambridge in 1865. He was ordained in 1871, the same year that he married Katherine Fowler. After his ordination he became a schoolmaster at Reading Grammar School and in 1873 he became Headmaster of Queen's School, Basingstoke. When Arthur Rutty arrived at St. John's he was thirty-seven years old, had two children, Arthur and Gilbert, aged eleven and ten respectively, and had been the successful Headmaster of a smaller school for a decade.

Arthur Rutty quickly set about expanding the intake of the School. In

1887 he proposed the establishment of the Supplementary Foundation where sons of clergy who could afford some fee contribution would be taken into the School with parents paying a portion of fees, to be decided by the committee. At the same time the Headmaster simplified the arrangements for non-clergy children. Until now the handful of non-clergy children paying fees were the private pupils of the Headmaster and thus not really members of St. John's School at all. Arthur Rutty gave up his private pupils and these were absorbed into the wider community of the School. By the early 1890s St. John's School had a broad range of pupils comprising full Foundationers, supplementary Foundationers and private fee-paying students. One of Arthur Rutty's main ambitions had been realised.

While seeking to broaden the intake of the School, Arthur Rutty set about creating a sixth form. The parents of bright Foundationers and supplementary Foundationers could apply for bursaries which would provide a further two years of education at St. John's. Even some less able Foundationers stayed on past sixteen provided their parents could fund the final years of school. When this group was supplemented by the increasing numbers of private fee-payers who had no problem paying for a sixth form education, St. John's had a viable sixth form by the middle of the 1890s. In 1899 the Sixth Form was divided into a commercial and a classical side. It was possible to gain 'extension' bursaries – bursaries to fund the Sixth Form – for either. The commercial side prepared boys for a life in business; the classical side prepared them for university entrance. To complement this considerable activity, wealthy patrons of the School were encouraged to offer scholarships and bursaries in connection with Oxford and Cambridge Colleges. Some of these generous benefactors were the same people who had had their original offers rejected by the committee a decade earlier.

In 1892 – after less than a decade of Arthur Rutty's Headmastership – there were 264 pupils in the School: 113 of them were full Foundationers, 81 supplementary Foundationers, 31 part Foundationers (usually boys remaining in the Sixth Form), 26 were fee-paying boarders and 13 were fee-paying day boys. In the same year 15 Old Johnians were attending Cambridge University. The achievement was extraordinary. Yet the

Headmaster remained dissatisfied with the number of full fee-paying pupils in the School – 39 out of 264. He had already embarked upon an ambitious building programme and fee income was an essential pre-requisite for expansion. He suggested to the committee that the School needed to change its name. It was still titled: 'St. John's Foundation School for the Sons of Poor Clergy'. He believed the title was off-putting to potential fee-paying parents. It took him nearly a decade to convince the committee that the phrase 'for the Sons of Poor Clergy' had to go. When it did go, at the turn of the century, it was allowed to remain on all correspondence with the donors to the charitable foundation.

The issue of the 'Sons of Poor Clergy' phrase illustrates a key problem which confronted the School now it was realising ambitions to become a public school. The School had promoted the fact that it was drawing its pupils from a single category of parent characterised by its relative poverty. The School suffered a double disadvantage here for it was not able to fund expansion through fee income and it offered little by way of upward social mobility to those who might be prepared to pay a fee. The establishment of Bradfield had strong similarities with St. John's – the same period with a clergyman founder keen to provide an Anglican education – but by 1859 Bradfield included amongst its pupils the two sons of the popular novelist, Anthony Trollope. The School was fashionable within a decade of its foundation. Through its commitment to *free* education for *poor* clergymen's sons, St. John's could never be fashionable. Arthur Rutty realised the problem and thus saw the necessity of changing the image of the School.

The creation of the Sixth Form helped him here too. In the centenary history of Malvern, one of its former distinguished Headmasters, William Grundy, is described as having been educated at Rossall. No mention is given to the eight years he spent at St. John's in receipt of a free education. Similarly, Sir Anthony Hope is always described as having been educated at Marlborough – rarely is there any mention of his five years at St. John's. The failure to have an outlet to Oxford and Cambridge colleges inevitably reduced the School's chances of gaining influence and reputation. Once a steady flow of Johnians was attending the universities the School's reputation rose.

The impression created so far might be of an ambitious teaching staff pitched against a reactionary school committee whose collective face seemed set against change. This would not be entirely fair. In fact one of the first voices to suggest broadening the School's intake – as early as the mid-1860s – was the influential banker, Peter Cazenove. It was a topic he raised consistently at committee meetings: he did have some support but he was always overruled by the majority. The committee did have a commitment to safeguard the terms of the charity: the Foundation had been established to provide free education, board and lodging for the sons of poor clergymen and the interests of those who had given to the charity for that purpose had to be safeguarded. Another factor is that the committee were mainly substantial men of business, Victorian philanthropists drawn into charitable work as a matter of duty. Most of them had plenty of other commitments, both commercial and charitable. Gordon Clark, for example, though a key member of the committee, was a governor of several other schools, including Cranleigh. These were very busy men giving generously of their time. Most of them, seeing their role as safeguarding the interests of the Foundation, were naturally wary of anything that might divert funds away from the purpose of the charity or might involve them in lengthy and expensive legal wrangles.

It is noticeable though that the committee appeared much more amenable to change under Arthur Rutty than it had done under Edwards Hawkins. The new Headmaster might have possessed stronger persuasive powers. But he was also the Headmaster of a now relatively large school. A school the size of St. John's in the 1890s could not be sustained by charitable donations. Fee income was essential in a way it had not been under Edwards Hawkins. Once the School had to appeal seriously to non-clergy parents it had to offer the facilities and quality of education that existed in schools which were now its competitors. This meant, amongst many other factors, a substantial building programme. Buildings were expensive and so more fee income had to be generated to fund them. In short, Arthur Rutty set in motion a spiral of expansion which needed to be supported by everyone involved in the School, both the committee and the academic staff.

If St. John's was to compete as a public school it needed to absorb the prevailing ethos of 'muscular Christianity'. It needed to take its sports more seriously. Since the move to Leatherhead in 1872 the School had developed strong rugby and cricket teams and played competitively against several schools, although the absence of sixth form pupils prevented the establishment of a sporting reputation. Arthur Rutty was an enthusiastic sportsman and wished to develop a sporting prowess alongside an academic one; indeed, like so many of his age, he saw the two as interconnected. Sadly for some, Arthur Rutty did not see the School's sporting future in the triumphs of the rugby field. He was a soccer man and in 1885 turned St. John's from a rugby school into a soccer one. The reason for this is not entirely clear. One of his own sons had been quite seriously injured in an accident on the rugby field soon after he arrived at Leatherhead. This might have been one reason for the change: his son was only twelve at the time which might have made the Headmaster question the appropriateness of rugby as a game for young-sters. The school from which he came had played soccer and, perhaps most important, he was a soccer player of some note himself, having played at both Merchant Taylors and Pembroke College, Cambridge. Indeed, the inaugural soccer match at St. John's in 1885 involved the Headmaster himself taking to the field. There was some early resistance to 'the dribbling game' as some called it, with illicit rugby games taking place around the premises and small boys acting as sentries − shouting 'Cave' when a master approached. This resistance soon waned when the School began to have huge sporting triumphs. In 1886 the 1st XI had an unbeaten season − this was only the second year of soccer being played in the School. By 1890 four Old Boys had played for their counties and by 1914 five had played for their country.

The summer game, of course, was cricket − a sport which Arthur Rutty supported as keenly as soccer. The Rutty family were all strong cricketers − Arthur Rutty's eldest son went on to play for Surrey. In 1890 the School appointed its first cricket professional, Mr. Mountford. Enthusiasm for 'the noblest game' was eloquently expressed in the May 1890 edition of 'The Johnian'. 'It is not generally considered how greatly the game shows the development of the national character: for to become a fine player requires broad open shoulders, strong arms, speed of limb, untiring patience, calculation, a promptitude in action, all of which we Englishmen claim, whether rightly or wrongly, to possess.'

By the late 1880s the School was playing a large number of schools at both its major sports.

Aldenham, Christ's Hospital, Cranleigh, Epsom, Highgate, Hurstpierpoint, King's College School, Lancing, Merchant Taylors and Whitgift were the leading opponents. Christ's Hospital has been a particularly long-standing sporting opponent whose association with St. John's went back to the Clapton period. Though Christ's Hospital might have been a far grander charitable undertaking there was the same commitment to the children of poor clergy and the same 'lack of status' in the early years meaning exclusion from the public school network; and there was a proximity of location which meant travel between the two schools was relatively easy (Christ's Hospital remained located in the City of London till 1902). The link with Merchant Taylors was probably due to Arthur Rutty's personal influence − he was an active Old Boy of the school who became President of its Old Boys' Association. He was a pupil at the school under Dr. Hessey who had been an active member of the St. John's committee. (Thought might be given here to the difficulties of the away fixture. There were frequent complaints from pupils about the exhaustion they felt after a long train journey home from a distant school. Schools which travelled particularly great distances to play each other would very often be provided with overnight accommodation.)

Alongside school fixtures the School also played a number of local clubs at both soccer and cricket. When playing local clubs the School would put out a team comprising a mixture of staff and students. Several masters at St. John's were outstanding games players − so the combined staff/student teams were indeed awesome. In 1891 a local cricket club requested the School play without the staff; 'The Johnian' bemoaned this fact: 'This year we are going to play without the aid of masters which will be a serious drawback.'

By 1890 St. John's was a key member of a network of public schools which played each other in a number of competitive sports. A great deal of significance was attached to this: it was a measurement of status. When competitive games is used as a criterion St..John's was clearly a public school of some standing by the early 1890s.

The building at Leatherhead had been designed for a capacity of 100 pupils. When Edwards Hawkins resigned in 1883 there were 140 pupils in the School. He had added just two buildings to the original School house – the Chapel in 1877 and the Infirmary in 1881. It was obviously essential that a building programme be put in place if the School was to provide adequate accommodation for the growing numbers. A school architect was appointed, R. Creese Harrison, and in 1885 the first part of the expansion programme commenced. This was an extension to the school house – an added wing opposite the Chapel. There was some concern at the proposed cost of the wing – £7,000 – but eventually the architect was given permission to proceed. In 1889 the school building was extended further with additional wings being created behind the Dining Hall (now the Assembly Hall/West House) and Big School (now Surrey House/West House). While these additions to the main building were being constructed the Headmaster was putting forward to the committee ambitious plans for new buildings. At a cost of £7,000 each Blocks A and B (North House/Montgomery House and Churchill House respectively) were constructed in 1891 and 1894. Also, in 1891, a new gymnasium was built (it became the Anthony Hope Theatre). As early as 1892 Arthur Rutty was planning his very special project – a grand Dining Hall. The first estimates for the cost of this building exceeded £20,000 and struck horror into the hearts of several members of the committee. Two of them proposed a motion: 'Having regard to the fact that St. John's is supported by public subscription the committee were not justified in incurring the large expenditure which would be involved in accepting any of these tenders.' The project was put on hold. Arthur Rutty told the committee that if he got permission to proceed with building Block B he could manage – for a while – without his Dining Hall. Block B duly went ahead while Arthur Rutty succeeded in getting a reduced estimate for the Dining Hall – £13,000. The building of the Dining Hall went ahead in 1898 (in fact it was to cost just under £15,000).

So at the turn of the century the buildings which we recognise today as St. John's School, Leatherhead, had just about taken shape. It had been a remarkable undertaking. In the region of £40,000 had been spent on the construction of 'the quad' (though in literal terms, the quad was not to be completed until 1998). The land purchased at Leatherhead in 1867 had cost £2,500 and the school building erected in 1872 just over £12,000. The sums of money Arthur Rutty and the committee spent in the 1890s were riches undreamt of a decade earlier. The heavy investment in bricks and mortar, though, did impose a financial burden upon the School and all those involved in it. It was now essential for the School to expand and to seek further income from fees.

It may be an appropriate moment in the narrative to pause and consider a rather less congenial aspect of St. John's during these years of expansion. The increased numbers using the buildings did create one unsavoury side-effect – diseases and smells. In 1886 Speech Day was cancelled due to an outbreak of measles, and throughout the early history of the School – well into the 1920s – there are references to epidemics of scarlet fever and mumps as well as tonsillitis and measles. In this regard St. John's was no different to any other boarding school. But in 1892 matters became serious when a local doctor recommended a potential parent to avoid St. John's because of its 'notorious' reputation for disease! In the same year a parent withdrew his son and demanded a reimbursement of fees because of the 'amount of disease' at the School. In 1893 a committee was established to consider these problems – it included, appropriately, the school doctor – and it was decided a completely new drainage system was needed: the old drainage system was serving twice as many people for whom it had been designed. Additionally the sanatorium sister was dismissed and the committee ordered that the sanatorium be 'regularly disinfected and washed down each week with carbolic.' The school doctor also insisted on the purchase of a 'disinfecting machine' at a cost of £110. In 1894, with complaints still being received from parents, the School closed down for the summer term while there was a complete cleansing of all drains and a scrubbing down of the whole school. Arthur Rutty rented a schoolroom at St. Mark's School, Windsor, for boys who were taking external examinations; everyone else had a very long summer break – April till August.

Any thought that this drastic action might have resolved the issue was shattered in 1898 when the Headmaster received a letter from the County Surveyor. He was, he wrote, responding to a petition from the residents of Leatherhead who were complaining about 'bad smells around the school property'. It was realised that the smells came from the school cesspool. The cesspool was a very large tank dug into the ground but left open to the elements. It was located some distance from the school building in a corner of the junior field. The County Medical Officer insisted that the cesspool be filled in. The problem was largely – but not totally – resolved in 1909 when the School was connected to the main sewage system of the town. There is a tendency to measure the history of a school through the tenure of office of its Headmaster. 1909 saw a new Headmaster at St. John's but it also witnessed the arrival of a mains sewage system. It is questionable which was the more significant event.

The 'sewage affair' came at an embarrassing time for the developing school – just at the moment when the building programme was at its most intensive. It did have an impact on the crucial fee-paying parent and there was, for the first time, a reduction in the number of fee-paying pupils applying for places. This was a temporary setback, however, and by 1898 the School's roll was expanding in the manner the Headmaster wanted. (In fact there was briefly a deliberate reducing of the School's size as a consequence of the problems revealed by the sewage crisis.)

In 1892 the School took on another characteristic of the public school – the house system. The Houses were developed purely for sporting competitions. Until now boys had played sports amongst themselves in informal teams – with the coming of the Houses a structure was established. There were, extraordinarily, nine Houses and where a boy was placed depended on the region from which he came. The system proved unwieldy and was simplified two years later when the nine Houses were reduced to four – North, South, East and West – again based on from which part of the country the boy originated. A series of sporting competitions was established and the House which was overall winner was termed the 'Cock House'. Houses, though, were not to have any sense of location for another twenty years. It was only then that a real sense of House loyalty was developed encompassing issues beyond the gamesfield. (In fact a clear sense of location was not really established till 1962 when North occupied Block A and South, East, West and Surrey had their locations rationalised.)

In 1886, two institutions were established which were to have a profound impact on the community of the School – 'The Johnian' magazine and the Old Johnian Club. The magazine in its early years appeared six times a year and was full of details of clubs, sporting achievements, articles and poems. To the school historian this new voice opens up a fresh insight on St. John's – before 'The Johnian' the only sources were the minute book of the committee and the Annual Report supplemented by the occasional written reminiscence. After 1886 it is possible to get a broader picture of life at the School. The portrait of the Johnian pupil which emerges from the magazine, however, is of a very staunch and conservative fellow: if only a study of school graffiti at the time were possible. 'The Johnian', though, does show a very active community with a great deal going on. In the early years there is a keenness to have new institutions and facilities. From 'The Johnian' comes the demand for new fives courts; from 'The Johnian' comes the demand for a tuck shop – and later, the demand for a rifle club. These requests invariably concluded with the phrase 'as happens in other Public Schools.' The Johnian certainly saw himself as a public schoolboy. The Old Boys' Association began in the same year and really for the same purpose – to be like other public schools. The subscription was ten shillings a year for which a member received all the school magazines, a ticket to the annual dinner and a list of members. The Old Johnian Club, after some early teething problems, was to become an institution of considerable significance in the development of the School. In 1891 another significant event occurred to strengthen the School's identity – the committee approved the school motto – 'Quae sursum sunt quaerite'[1] – which was duly engraved on the archway of Block B.

Arthur Rutty retired in 1909. He became Rector of Lyminge near

---

[1] 'Seek those things which are above.' (St. Paul's letter to the Colossians, chapter 3, verse 1).

Folkestone where he died ten years later at the age of 73. The St. John's which he bequeathed his successor was an established public school of some repute. While maintaining its loyalty to the clergyman's son, it was also now a school attracting the children of the prosperous middle class. Arthur Rutty's achievement was outstanding. It is no exaggeration to say that he had created an English public school.

CHAPTER SEVEN

Fire and War: Tribulations 1913–1918

ARTHUR RUTTY'S SUCCESSOR IN 1909 WAS THE REVEREND Edmund Downes. He was just thirty-one years of age, a graduate of University College, Oxford who had spent his early teaching career at Wellington. A strong, powerful man of huge physique – he was a swimming blue – he and his young wife made an enormous, and favourable, impact upon the School when they arrived. Unfortunately, the early period of Edmund Downes' headmastership was to be overshadowed by two disasters – the School fire in June 1913, and, of course, the Great War 1914-1918.

In the early morning of 9 June 1913 the School was awoken by the ringing of the school bell indicating a fire alarm. A fire had broken out on the top corridor of the main school building and had quickly spread into the two dormitory wings at each end of the building. The boys in the west wing were fortunately able to descend the stairs and escape into the quadrangle but those in the east wing were stranded when the stair-case went up in flames: they had to escape by descending from the windows by chutes. Within a couple of hours the whole school building was ablaze and fire services from as far away as Guildford were being used to extinguish the flames. The noise of the fire caused such uproar that many citizens of the town arose from bed to watch the drama. The damage caused was devastating. The whole of the main school building was virtually destroyed with just the shell, remarkably, remaining intact.

There was, extraordinarily, no loss of life or injury except for a fireman who tripped on his hose and needed a few stitches in his head. (This did not, of course, prevent the famous myth of the Fireman's Ghost – a story which haunted many a new boy for several generations).

The cause of the fire was never explained to total satisfaction, although a reasonably accurate account can probably now be given. The fire broke out in a study-bedroom of one of the masters, Charles Cole. He lived in a room in the middle of the top corridor of the main school building. On the night of the fire Charles Cole was actually in the Infirmary because he was unwell – a victim perhaps of the measles epidemic in the School. His room was thus empty. After the fire he took legal proceedings 'against the parents of the boys in respect of the balance of loss through the fire'. This would suggest that boys had gained entry to his room and the fire had come about due to activities conducted in the room by these boys. The committee, incidentally, seem to have persuaded Mr. Cole not to proceed with his case – they did, in fact, pay him compensation themselves as they did all the other masters who lost possessions. Charles Cole might not have been pleased with the manner of his treatment after the fire for he never returned to teach at the School and went to live in France. The Headmaster, of course, launched an enquiry into the causes of the fire and as a conse- quence one boy was publicly beaten and expelled though it was clear several others were involved. The expelled boy was in fact the boy who gave the first alarm; in the early press reports he was treated as a hero. The event received enormous publicity making the front page of the national newspapers.

There was much speculation in both the local and national press about the cause of the fire. Two days earlier the Derby had taken place four miles away on Epsom Downs. It was the notorious Derby where the suffragette, Emily Davison, threw herself in front of the King's horse – killing the horse and sustaining injuries from which she soon died. There was widespread alarm of further outrage and for a while the fire at St. John's was suspected of being such a suffragette activity. Alas, the culprits were closer to home.

This was, naturally, an incident which lived long in the memories of the boys in the School at the time and there are many eyewitness accounts. Two vivid descriptions are given below: one by Philip Shenton, twelve years old at the time and able to observe from the distance of Block B; the other by Charles Morley aged fourteen who was at the centre of events.

Philip Shenton wrote: 'I was a junior sleeping in a B block dormitory and assembled with the rest of the school on the sacred lawn of the Quad where we sat in small groups to watch the Fire Brigade at work . . . The centre two main wings housing the two large senior dormitories above the main Assembly Hall and Library below were completely gutted . . . The cause of the fire was a bit of a mystery at first and the boy who first raised the alarm was praised as a hero in the press. It transpired later that he had caused the fire. He had gone into this master's room, and had spilt some whisky on the carpet. In a fit of guilty desperation he had put a match to the spilled spirits and gone to bed. However, he must have lost his nerve and raised the alarm. Subsequently he lost his nerve still further and ran away . . . He was caught and brought back to be publicly caned in front of the whole school before being expelled. This was the only public thrashing by the Head which I ever witnessed'.

Charles Morley: 'I went to bed as usual on Sunday night . . . It seemed to me as if I had been to sleep about half-an-hour when I thought I was dreaming because I heard voices and then I heard the bell going . . . I sat up and found the dormitory already half-dressed. There was smoke coming along the passage; it was quite dark but luckily the light was on. We were all getting fairly excited now and were wondering where the fire was starting. The bell kept tolling . . . We got down by staircase as the fire had not reached it yet. One of the big dormitories on the other side of the building had to come down by chute . . . When we got into the quadrangle we saw the whole of one of the masters' sitting rooms was ablaze. The school hose was turned on but not to much effect . . . Various brigades arrived soon but they were unable to check the rapid progress of the fire. The fire got a firm grip on the building and at last reached the two big dormitories which with the big schoolroom and the Library formed the whole of the wing of the building . . . Most of us had got nothing left except what we had hastily put on in the dormitory . . .

The damage estimated done to the school is £20,000 . . . The origin of the fire is unknown but enquires are being made.'

Notable items of expense for the committee were the purchase of new books for the Library and new uniforms for the Officer Training Corps. The OTC not only lost all its uniforms but also all its ammunition – a key moment in the fire was the explosion caused when the fire reached the ammunition depot.

Three houses in and around Leatherhead were rented to provide accommodation for boys. The 'Leatherhead Institute' was hired to provide a teaching area and the Dining Hall served as a giant classroom as well as a centre for nourishment. With these arrangements in place the School opened up again for most boys on 4 July (though some did not return till September). A noticeable victim of the fire was the Headmaster whose house had been entirely gutted. (The Headmaster's house comprised the first two floors of the west wing of the main building – today's West House and Common Room area). The committee thought it an appropriate opportunity to provide the Headmaster with Copthorne, the neighbouring house which had been purchased as an investment some years earlier; fortunately there were no tenants in Copthorne at the time so Edmund Downes and his family were able to move in with little delay. Eventually an extensive rebuilding programme for the whole main building was put into operation. The insurance company agreed a figure of £10,000 which covered most of its cost.

The School was still experiencing the practical consequences of the fire when events in the outside world began to make an impact. In fact the official re-opening of the main building by the Duchess of Albany (Queen Victoria's daughter-in-law) took place on 1 July 1914 – three days after the assassination of Archduke Franz Ferdinand at Sarajevo and five weeks before England declared war on Germany. In the weeks before the outbreak of the war there were frequent debates and discussions in the School about the threatening clouds in eastern Europe – although the chief preoccupation at the time was the illness which was raging throughout the School community, measles and mumps epidemics occurring simultaneously. The School was very suddenly made aware of the reality of war in August when the first recorded death in combat of an officer was that of an Old Johnian, Joseph Gedge, killed in the North Sea on 6 August (two days after war was declared) when his ship, HMS Amphion, hit a German mine.

Statistically the consequence of the Great War on the School was enormous. Of nearly 800 Old Boys who fought in the war, 154 were killed and 143 were seriously wounded. Two Johnians were awarded the Victoria Cross, Geoffrey Woolley and Eric Robinson. In addition 9 DSOs were won and 56 Military Crosses. Geoffrey Woolley, on top of his VC, was also awarded the Croix de Guerre, as were three other Johnians. In the totality of horror and bravery it would be wrong to highlight individual situations but there are particularly poignant stories. The Beechey brothers, Bernard and Frank, sons of a Lincoln clergyman, joined the 9th Lincolnshire Regiment in 1914. Bernard had won an Exhibition to St. John's College, Cambridge, in 1899 and subsequently became a schoolmaster. He volunteered at the relatively late age of 33 and was killed at Ypres just a year later in September 1915. His younger brother, Frank, died on the Somme a year afterwards. They had two other brothers, Charles and Harold, who did not come to St. John's; they too were killed during the War. So Thomas and Amy Beechey lost all four sons in the course of the War. Cecil Roberts, an outstanding athlete at the School, played football for his country, Wales, in 1914 and had a sparkling career ahead of him. He was killed on the Western Front in 1917. Victor Bedwell, athlete and scholar, went up to Exeter College, Oxford, a year before the outbreak of war. As soon as he was awarded his first class honours degree he joined the Suffolk regiment. He was killed in France in 1917. His father wrote to the School to say that before his son proceeded to the Front he had made a will and left £25 to the School Library. Charles Morley, the fourteen-year-old boy whose vivid description of the Great Fire has just been recounted, was killed in France in 1918.

One of the most poignant stories, though, is that of someone who never actually left Leatherhead during the course of the War. Lancelot Driffield left St. John's in 1899 to take up an exhibition at St. Catherine's College, Cambridge. An outstanding games player, he won blues at both cricket and soccer and went on to play cricket for Northamptonshire.

He returned to his old school to teach in 1911 when he was thirty – having spent his first teaching years at St. Edmund's, Canterbury. He was appointed the first Contingent Commander of the Officers' Training Corps soon after his arrival. He was appointed Housemaster of East House in 1912. He was a popular and kindly man who was held in high respect. Philip Shenton recalled: 'Our Housemaster was Mr. Driffield, a very fine youngish man who had been awarded two blues… He was tremendously popular.' Another old boy, Penry Whiteford, recalled 'a kindly and friendly man' at a time when the school was not really noted for such virtues.

Lancelot Driffield was a huge success as Contingent Commander of the OTC, so much so that he was asked to lecture to regular soldiers and volunteers on rifle drill. A battalion of the Royal Fusiliers was billetted in Leatherhead and 'Big School' was used as a lecture room for them. In 1915 the annual inspection of the OTC impressed the Inspecting Officer so much that the Chairman of the committee was requested to write to Mr. Driffield to congratulate him on his achievement.

With all this military involvement Lancelot Driffield was aware of the fact he was only really playing at being a soldier. To lecture young recruits at the School was hardly the contribution expected of an intelligent and athletic man in his early thirties. He was conscious of the criticism levelled at him. In the first year of the War there was huge pressure placed on young men to volunteer – Britain, much to the dismay of its French ally, depended on volunteers to supplement its regulars with conscription not being introduced till 1916. Lancelot Driffield did volunteer but was turned down on health grounds: he had a heart murmur. Some did not believe that this tall, athletic Cambridge double blue and county cricketer could have been rejected for war service on health grounds. Lancelot Driffield had a difficult war. In October 1918, a month before the armistice, he collapsed and died at the top of the East House stairs. He was thirty-seven years old.

The School was naturally very proud of the two Johnians who were awarded VCs, Geoffrey Woolley and Eric Robinson. The following is part of the citation for Geoffrey Woolley's VC: 'Although the only officer on the hill at the time and with very few men he successfully resisted all attacks on his trenches and continued throwing bombs and encouraging his men till relieved. His trench all this time was being heavily shelled and bombed and was subjected to heavy machine gun by the enemy.' Geoffrey Woolley's heroics took place at Hill 60 on the Ypres Salient – a notorious scene of continuous conflict throughout the war. His award, the first territorial VC of the War, was given in recognition of 'his conspicuous bravery on Hill 60 during the night of April 20–April 21 1915.' (Each year the School visits the Battlefields of the Great War and an expedition is made to Hill 60 in honour of this courageous Johnian.) Geoffrey Woolley survived the War and went on to teach at Rugby and Harrow where he became Chaplain. His brother was the eminent archaeologist, Sir Leonard Woolley, who attended the School between 1890 and 1899.

Eric Robinson's courageous conduct occurred two months before Geoffrey Woolley's in February 1915, although it was not cited until August. He received his award for bravery at the Dardanelles campaign in Turkey. 'He advanced alone, under heavy fire, into an enemy's gun position and, destroying a four-inch gun, returned to his party for another charge . . . He would not allow members of his demolition party to accompany him as their white uniforms rendered them conspicuous.' Eric Robinson also survived the war and had a distinguished naval career, eventually retiring as a Vice-Admiral.

The War had a direct impact upon the life of the School. There were frequent references from the boys to the inadequate teaching staff – elderly teachers were brought in to replace the younger ones who had gone off to fight. Concerts no longer happened. Societies closed down. Suddenly the OTC had to be taken much more seriously – no longer the weekly afternoon session but three evening lectures and practical sessions per week in addition. There were football matches with the wounded Belgian soldiers recuperating in the town and the regulars of the Royal Fusiliers billetted locally. During the holidays the School was hired out to the army for the billetting of troops. The fine lawn of the quadrangle was dug up for the planting of potatoes. The committee offered reduced fees to the sons of officers killed in the War and several boys came to the School under this arrangement.

In September 1916 the boys watched from the dormitory windows as a Zeppelin flew slowly across the night sky – to be destroyed by the legendary air ace, William Leefe Robinson. As the War went on the lengthening litany of the fallen was read out in Chapel by the Headmaster. Senior boys would be particularly shocked when the names of those they remembered were called out, once prefects, actors, musicians, heroes of the 1st XI now lying dead on the fields of Flanders or the sands of Turkey. Penry Whiteford remembered the kindly Stanley Squires, a School prefect whose fag he had been and whose consideration had made his first days at St. John's at least bearable. Stanley Squires was killed at Gallipoli in 1915; when the Headmaster made the announcement, Penry was starting his Sixth Form career. He recalled that of the ten School prefects in 1911 when he went to the School five were killed during the course of the War.

Yet despite its catastrophic nature the War had less of a personal impact on the School than the measles epidemic which occurred in 1917 when six boys died. Philip Shenton lost his best friend, Sam Thursby, whose School number he remembered for the rest of his life – E100. 'The loss,' he wrote, 'affected the School more I think than the ever growing list of casualties in the fighting.' (Sam Thursby's father was Vicar of Castle Rising in Norfolk. Sam's body could not be transported home to Norfolk because of wartime travel restrictions. He was buried in Leatherhead Parish Church.)

On the evening of 11 November 1918 members of the School went to the huge bonfire outside the Old Bull Hotel to celebrate the end of hostilities. Seven months later, on 19 June 1919, the country officially recognised the end of the War with a public holiday. At Leatherhead the central point of celebrations was a grand lunch held for 350 returning servicemen and the host was the Headmaster, Edmund Downes, who was pleased to put the Dining Hall to such joyful – yet poignant – use.

St. Mark's Church, Hamilton Terrace
The School was founded here and the first pupils were taught in the curate's house next door.

Kilburn (Greville Mount House)

The School moved here in 1854 and remained till 1857.

Clapton House

The School moved here in 1859 and remained till the move to Leatherhead in 1872.

Construction workers on the foundations of the new Leatherhead building

Leatherhead

The School moved into a purpose-built school house in 1872. Here it was to remain and expand.

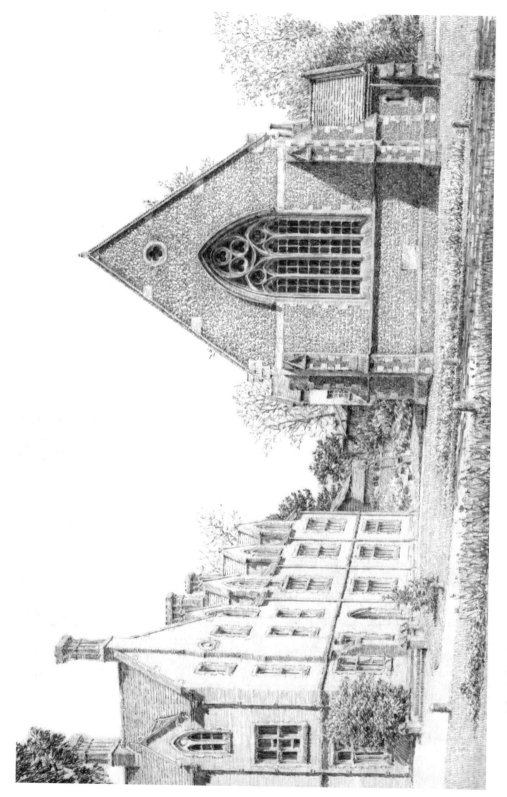

The School Chapel was built in 1877 and consecrated by the Bishop of Winchester. It remained the Chapel till 1962.

Revd Anthony Thomson
The curate of St. Mark's, Hamilton Terrace, and first Headmaster of St. John's, 1851–1857.

Revd Edward Hawkins
The third Headmaster of St. John's, 1861–1883, who supervised the move to Leatherhead in 1872.

Revd Arthur Rutty
The fourth Headmaster of St. John's, 1883–1909, under whose direction the School expanded greatly.

Canon Edmund Audley Downes
The fifth Headmaster of St. John's, 1909–1932, had the fire, the Great War and the economic recession to contend with.

Jack Carter
The sixth Headmaster of St. John's, 1933–1947.
The first lay Headmaster who brought a warmth
and compassion to the School.

Hereward Wake
The seventh Headmaster of St. John's, 1948–1960,
under whom the School expanded and welcomed
Viscount Montgomery to the Governing Body.

Ian Sutherland
The eighth Headmaster of St. John's, 1960–1970,
scholar and cricketing enthusiast, who directed the
School in a turbulent decade.

Edward Hartwell
The ninth Headmaster of St. John's, 1970–1985,
under whom the School expanded enormously and
began to attract increasing numbers of day boys.

David Brown

The tenth Headmaster of St. John's, 1985–1992, under whose direction the School opened its door to Sixth Form girls.

Christopher Tongue

The eleventh Headmaster of St. John's, 1993-, under whose direction the School has undergone a further period of expansion.

Common Room 1940

Fire 1913

In June 1913 the main school building was devastated by a fire. National newspapers ran the story on their front pages.

Lancelot Driffield

Double Cambridge blue, county cricketer, housemaster of East House, Old Johnian, First Contingent Commander of the CCF. Died aged thirty-seven in East House, October 1918.

Sam Thursby

Son of the Vicar of Castle Rising, Norfolk, a popular boy who died in the measles epidemic, 1917. His school number was E100. He is buried in Leatherhead Church.

Dining Hall 1919

The School played host to a grand luncheon in honour of the men of Leatherhead safely returned from the Great War, June 1919.

School Mission

This mission was the inspiration of the Reverend Nathaniel Edwards MC, Old Johnian and vicar of St. John's, Walworth. It began in 1924 and continued till 1960.

Oxford Old Johnian Dinner, February 1929

The Headmaster, Canon Edmund Audley Downes, is seated second left. The Reverend Nathaniel Edwards, founder of the School Mission, is standing third from the right.

The Archbishop of Canterbury, Dr Cosmo Lang, gave the prizes at Speech Day in 1931. Behind him left, is the long serving Bursar, J.H. Burnside, and to his right (without the hat) the Revd. C.W. Ingram.

Monty: Speech Day, 1958

Field Marshal Montgomery enjoyed presiding at Speech Day. In 1958 the Guest of Honour was
General Lauris Norstad, the Supreme Commander, Allied Powers in Europe. To the right is
the Headmaster, Hereward Wake, and to the left the School Captain, M.T. Evans.

Aerial view of the School in the 1950s

CHAPTER EIGHT

Contrasting Styles and Fortunes: Edmund Downes and Jack Carter
1909–1947

FOR NEARLY FORTY YEARS THE FORTUNES OF THE SCHOOL were to be directed by two men who left their images firmly imprinted in its folklore. These images sharply conflict. Edmund Audley Downes (he always used the 'Audley' in his correspondence) was Headmaster from 1909 to 1932 and he bequeathed a reputation for iron discipline which in the eyes of some bordered on the brutal. He is immortalised in the nickname for all St. John's Headmasters – 'the Bod' – BOD standing for 'Bloody Old Downes'. Jack Carter, on the other hand, appeared to have no enemies – a much loved man. He was a sympathetic and caring bachelor, rather eccentric, who lived in Copthorne (the Headmaster's House) with his mother and sister. He wandered around the school with the tuckshop keys around his neck and was prepared to get on his hands and knees to assist with the scrubbing of the school floors if this was deemed necessary. Jack Carter was the first lay Headmaster – he was also the only St. John's Headmaster to move on to a further headship, at Blundell's School in Devon. These two very different men guided the School through a turbulent period involving two world wars, several epidemics, the near ruinous fire and severe economic recession. Their headships ended very differently – Edmund Downes quickly departed after giving the School barely a month's notice; Jack Carter went on to the headship of a bigger school. Yet there appears to be another side to the story of these significant men. Downes may have been the austere disciplinarian but he was also an energetic man devoted to the School and driven by a determination to create a St. John's Junior School. Jack Carter may have been the endearing eccentric but he had clear aims for the School and a drive and ambition to see these fulfilled.

If Edmund Downes' reputation was fearsome this was certainly not the picture when he arrived in 1909. He was thirty-one and his wife Muriel a year younger. They were an attractive young couple and Mrs. Downes in particular made an enormous – and very favourable – impact on the boys. An invitation to take tea with Mrs. Downes was greeted with considerable enthusiasm from sixth formers. (Her daughter was to receive similar, though somewhat less formal, attention from senior boys a generation later.) The Downes were more than thirty years younger than the departing Ruttys and the infusion of young blood into the Headmaster's House was noticed by many.

Yet it is clear this positive image did not last. While it is important to be wary of the anecdotes of Old Boys there can be no question that the School developed an image of tough discipline and austerity which the Headmaster came to epitomise. 'A sadist, a bully, a very stupid man', wrote one Old Boy in the 1980s showing that the years had not tempered his views. When a senior master wrote to the eminent man-of-letters, Geoffrey Grigson, in the 1960s, asking him to come and talk to the Sixth Form he received a very curt reply. Geoffrey Grigson, with his four brothers, had attended the School before and after the Great War and went on to become a poet and editor of distinction. He informed the hapless Derek Pitt, Head of History, that the sight of the Leatherhead postmark on the letter of invitation was sufficient to make him quiver and he never wanted to hear from the school again. (All Geoffrey Grigson's brothers were to be killed – two in combat and two in plane crashes.) But the most famous observation on the regime of Edmund Downes was that made by Leonard Wilson, the distinguished Bishop of Birmingham, who had attended the School just before the Great War. Leonard Wilson had been the Bishop of Singapore during the Second World War and was captured and tortured by the Japanese. After the war he converted to Christianity one of his captors. When he was asked how he had managed to survive a Japanese prisoner-of-war camp he said that the Japanese experience was nothing compared to what he had suffered at St. John's School, Leatherhead. Unfortunately, this remark made its way into the national press and has become the most celebrated comment on the Downes years.

It does seem apparent that Edmund Downes was liberal with the use of the cane and was quite happy for senior boys to beat juniors for offences as minor as missing choir practice. Old Boys recall squads of prefects roaming the junior Houses dispensing beatings for a variety of offences. Undoubtedly a regime was in place whose reliance on physical punishment seems barbaric by the standards of today. Yet corporal punishment remained widespread in schools until the 1980s; senior boys were beating junior boys in many public schools till well into the 1950s. In the context of the time Edmund Downes was no better or worse than many a public school Headmaster.

Perhaps more significant in explaining the toughness and austerity at St. John's – and perhaps the swift departure of the Headmaster in 1932 – was the failure to attract the non-clergy boy. In 1930 there were only thirty non-Foundationers in the School – seven of them day boys; this fell to twenty-four in 1931, eight of them day boys – barely ten per cent of the school population. This was a substantial reduction from the days of Arthur Rutty. With the numbers of non-Foundationers so small and actually declining St. John's seemed in danger of returning to its days as a charity school. Admittedly there was now a Sixth Form and an excellent site but the absence of the fee-paying parent meant shortage of funds – the School was in a permanent financial crisis throughout the 1920s and 1930s – and the lack of any real incentive to keep up with those prestigious schools it met on the gamesfield. Austerity – in the form of poor food and heating – was the inevitable consequence of the absence of fee income to boost the charitable foundation and it was this austerity which would make the School unattractive to the fee-paying parent. Arthur Rutty's upward spiral had turned into Edmund Downes' downward spiral.

Yet it would be unfair to lay the blame on Edmund Downes. His headmastership had experienced a number of setbacks which would have tested the most resilient of Headmasters. The 1913 fire had devastated the

School and not all the costs had been met through insurance. The horrors of the Great War soon afterwards had been a further enormous burden – and at the same time there were the devastating mumps, measles and influenza epidemics running through 1917, 1918 and 1919. A decade later came the Great Depression which struck an enormous blow to all independent schools. Edmund Downes was not lucky in the timing of his period of office. In addition, the committee of the School, faced with the circumstances of the economic recession, decided *more* free places needed to be offered to the sons of poor clergy as there were more cases than ever of severe hardship. So the School took in additional Foundationers thus further increasing expenditure while reducing potential income.

Despite the succession of problems during the Downes years there were a number of significant developments. The school acquired more land – four acres 'to the west of the Senior Field', the cricket pavilion areas, were purchased in 1912 and a further four acres from the Linden House estate in 1922. The School wanted to buy the whole estate but could not afford it – it paid £1,800 for the four acres. In 1920 the War Memorial was unveiled on the quadrangle at a ceremony conducted by H.H. Gordon Clark, Treasurer of the committee and High Sheriff of Surrey. In 1925 the swimming bath was constructed at a cost of £7,500, most of which was funded through the bequest of T.S. Whitaker with the balance being met by the War Memorial Fund.

In 1919 rugby football was restored as the main winter sport. Edmund Downes had never been a great soccer enthusiast but what seemed to have decided the issue was the number of other schools – many of them competitors – who were making the switch. The same outrage which greeted the demise of rugby in 1885 now greeted its re-introduction. Lookouts were posted as illegal soccer matches were played. But, as in 1885, criticism was quelled by the performance of the first team. The first ever St. John's soccer XI had won its first fixture – and so did the first rugby XV: they beat Christ's Hospital.

As soon as he became Headmaster Edmund Downes reorganised the House system. He gradually ended the arrangement whereby boys were placed in Houses according to the location of their home – northerners in North House, southerners in South House etc. He made it his job to place boys into Houses and these Houses were given locations in the main building with Housemasters resident in those areas. The House system as we recognise it today was the work of Edmund Downes.

The age of entry into the School was raised. In 1917 it was raised from nine to eleven (and in 1938 to thirteen). In 1930 the traditional system of selection to the School through election was abolished. The Headmaster and the committee now decided on who was eligible for the charitable Foundation. (A further significant development came in 1936 when the system of free and supplementary Foundationships was abolished. Five divisions of parental income were created with the poorest parent paying £15 per annum and the wealthiest £105).

An important change in the governing of the School took place in 1922 when the School was granted a Royal Charter. In this way the School governors became a 'Body Politic and Corporate with Perpetual Succession and a Common Seal.' In practical terms this meant that the School had a legal identity of its own and the Council of the School had full power to act for it – it is from this moment that the School 'committee' became the School 'Council'.

In 1924 the School Mission was established thanks to the initiative and energy of Nathaniel Edwards, an Old Boy who was the incumbent of St. John's, Walworth, a parish close to the Elephant and Castle in South London. Edwards, who won the Military Cross in the Great War, was a revered parish priest in Walworth and is still remembered there by elderly parishioners. He was keen to strengthen the link between his parish and his old school and the Mission very quickly became a major institution. Its central point was the annual visit to Leatherhead of the parishioners of Walworth who travelled to the School by train each Whit Monday to play cricket and tennis and perform reviews and concerts. There were Mission camps in the summer holidays where St. John's boys mixed with the children of the Walworth parish. The Mission continued until 1960 though it is generally recognised that some of the momentum left it after the untimely death of Edwards in 1935.

Edmund Downes' greatest ambition – his central project – was to establish a St. John's Junior School. He frequently put forward proposals to the Council only to have them rejected. It was unfortunate that he was trying to establish his Junior School at the time of the Depression when the Council felt they could not countenance costly projects and were in fact falling back on their core constituent, the full Foundationer. It was, indeed, the Foundationer that Edmund Downes was trying to help. One of the difficulties for the clergyman was – and is – how to fund education before coming to St. John's. As the age of entry to the School had risen so the problem for the clergymen grew. Downes' solution was a Junior School for ages eight to thirteen. He failed to achieve this but what he did set in motion was a scheme which would reap dividends for his successors. He proposed the extension of the Foundation into a number of preparatory schools willing to join the scheme. In this way a boy aged nine whose clergyman father committed him to St. John's would receive a place at a preparatory school for greatly reduced fees – usually half the full fees but sometimes less. By the middle of the 1930s 150 boys were in receipt of subsidised preparatory school education and over 60 preparatory schools were involved in the scheme. It seems typical of Edmund Downes' fortune that this imaginative scheme – largely inspired by his wife, as he always admitted – bore him scant reward but served his successors well.

The demise of Edmund Downes was sudden. The Johnian recorded: 'He presented his last sermon as Headmaster in the School Chapel on October 30 and left the next day to be instituted to the Rectory of Hadleigh on November 2.' Edmund Downes had placed his letter of resignation with the Council in September 1932 and requested that the usual term's notice not be asked of him because the Archbishop of Canterbury wanted him to take up his position as Rector of Hadleigh in Suffolk immediately. The Council's willingness to agree to this unusual request – in the middle of term – would suggest that there was no great sorrow at their parting with him. Rumours have abounded about the swift mid-term departure of the Headmaster. There had been an incident involving a fight among senior boys where one of them had ended up in hospital. The new Medical Officer, a young GP, Alan Everett (whose son became Headmaster of Tonbridge School), had expressed concern to members of the Council about the prevalence of physical punishment. At the same time as Edmund Downes resigned, the school's Bursar, J.H. Burnside, who also had an extensive teaching timetable, was told to take a three-month rest because of mental exhaustion (on the insistence of Alan Everett). It is clear all was not well at the end of 1932. But the reason for the departure of Edmund Downes may have had little to do with skulduggery. He was heavily involved in the new diocese of Guildford, recently formed from part of the massive Winchester diocese, and had become one of the first honorary canons. It was rumoured that he might have been selected as the first Bishop of Guildford and was upset when this did not happen. Several Council members were unhappy about the amount of time Edmund Downes spent on diocesan issues and had made their views known. This, together with the obvious fact that the School was not expanding and not attracting fee-paying parents, probably explains why a swift departure suited both parties. Mr. Coddington became Acting Headmaster while the Council sought a replacement for Canon Downes. John Somers Carter, aged 31, was appointed and he took up his post in January 1933.

Jack Carter's brief was clear: to make the School a more humane location, eradicate the image of oppression, and draw in a wider range of pupils. He was largely successful in all three aims – though not before there was considerable concern about the financial well-being of the School. When he left in 1947 to take on the headship of Blundell's, there was considerable dismay at his departure amongst all elements of the School community. Though the Depression dominated the first part of his headship and the Second World War the latter, Jack Carter's direction of the School was mostly a happy and fruitful period of advance though a narrow tightrope had been walked.

John Somers Carter was a classicist from Balliol College, Oxford. His father had been Rector of Edinburgh Academy and later Headmaster of Bedford School and Jack had attended both schools. After graduating from Oxford he had taught at Cheltenham College where he became a Junior Housemaster.

Despite the precarious School finances, Jack Carter's first action was to request funding for a new classroom block. He was appalled at the teaching facilities in the School and informed the Council that no advances could be made until the School had adequate classrooms. An appeal was launched to raise the £25,000 needed to build a modern classroom facility. The funding of the building in the midst of the Depression was a bold undertaking but, whatever misgivings were expressed at the time, it reaped a dividend. When the Classroom Block opened in 1935 – with its sixteen classrooms and four laboratories – St. John's had a facility which put it on a par with other public schools. Just as important, it released accommodation in the main school building which could be used to improve residential and recreational facilities for both pupils and staff. In addition, the School began to buy several homes in the locality – 'Devonia', opposite the School, Paddock House and a small property in Poplar Road. (In 1946 the School built onto Paddock House to create a further staff house). Jack Carter, bachelor though he was, saw the need to make the School more friendly to married masters; he saw the provision of family accommodation as an essential prerequisite. All this cost money which the School could ill afford and for a time it did seem that Jack Carter's plans might have stretched resources beyond the limit. In 1935 the Council reported 'they have succeeded in placing the school in the position of an up-to-date public school but they have so far been unsuccessful in placing the finances of the school on a sounder basis.' The appeal for the funding of the Classroom Block initially raised only £16,000 – two-thirds of the cost – and there was still £2,000 owing at the outbreak of the War. But the property expansion did continue – in 1943 the School purchased the large house opposite the School, 'Windfield', for £11,000 from the Still family. (E.R. Still, Chairman of the Council between 1918 and 1930, had married the daughter of Charles Churchill, the philanthropist who had arranged the removal of the School from Hamilton Terrace and who was the first Chairman of the committee. He had died in 1931.) The intention of the School was at first to resurrect the idea of a preparatory school and locate it in the building but this idea was soon abandoned. In fact the 'Windfield' purchase was a constant headache for the School which never really worked out what to do with it. It was leased for a time to Leatherhead Hospital, then to a vacuum cleaner manufacturer; an ambitious proposal to place all the day boys in it was rejected on the grounds of expense;

part of the estate was compulsorily purchased by Leatherhead Urban District Council for the building of old people's bungalows – this reduced its attraction as a school facility. In 1961 it was sold to New Ideal Homes Ltd. for £151,000 – so it had probably been a wise investment despite the difficulties.

Another important development in the middle of the 1930s was the reorganisation of the administration of the School. Until 1935 it had been a cumbersome and time-consuming arrangement. The bureaucratic organisation of the School was run from an office in Victoria Street in central London. The Headmaster travelled up once a fortnight to discuss issues of administration, from the pay of staff to the price of fresh meat. Edmund Downes had seen the absurdity of the situation and had transferred many operations to the School, but still key decisions were made in Victoria Street by the Secretary. A bursar, based at Leatherhead, had been appointed in 1917 but he was a long-serving member of the academic staff, J.H. Burnside, who had an extensive teaching programme alongside his bursarial responsibility. The key decisions were made by the Secretary in London. In 1935 Jack Carter achieved something Edmund Downes had always wanted – the closing down of the London office and the transfer of all administration to Leatherhead. In addition the dual Bursar-Secretary role was combined into a single appointment. No longer did the Headmaster have to travel up to Victoria to settle the affairs of the School.

The heavy investment in the middle 1930s – together with the undoubted personality of the Headmaster – at last began to make an impact on School numbers and by 1938 they had reached 250 and, crucially, 60 of these were non-Foundationers. St. John's was once more beginning to attract fee-paying parents. It had been a close run thing. In 1937 a member of the Council, Alexander Abel Smith, a director of Schroders Bank, had been asked to use his City connections to find a 'sponsor' for the School. The Vintners Company had expressed an interest in taking over the School and offering charitable provision to their associates alongside the sons of clergymen. The scheme was not pursued but the fact that discussions were undertaken did indicate the depth of concern being felt about the School's future. The collapse of the scheme might be a source of regret – a school comprising the sons of vicars and the sons of wine merchants sounds a jolly institution.

As the School's fortunes began to turn it was decided to open a fifth house – in 1937 – to relieve some of the crowding in the main building. Block 'B' had been the junior school where boys stayed till they joined their senior House. This arrangement ended and Block B became Churchill House – named in recognition of the family who had done so much for the development of the School since its foundation. Its first Housemaster was G.L. Gettins.

At the outbreak of the War in 1939 the School was in better condition than it had been for many years. The War was obviously going to create a new set of difficulties but the School was at last structurally sound with growing numbers and a good mix of pupils. Jack Carter, in his distinct manner, had pushed forward a programme of modernisation and expansion in the most testing of circumstances. One or two members of the Council might have seen the Headmaster as profligate, some might have despaired at the School's future, but as a body they stood by the Headmaster and worked with him to improve the School. When Jack Carter moved on to Blundells at the end of 1947 there were 300 boys in the School – one half of them were the sons of clergy and the other half were fee-paying bourgeoisie; it was the model constituency of which Arthur Rutty would have been proud.

CHAPTER NINE

The Teachers and
the Taught II

JACK CARTER'S SUCCESSOR, HEREWARD WAKE, WAS TO ASSUME direction of a school which had come through a period of great difficulty but was now able to face the future with some confidence. But the future in 1948 was not easy to fathom. The Education Act of 1944 and the Labour election landslide a year later caused foreboding in the independent sector. It did seem, maybe, by 1948 that public schools were 'safe' at least for the foreseeable future. St. John's, anyway, always felt some assurance that its commitment to the free education of clergymen's sons would stand it in good stead in a hostile political climate.

Some months after Hereward Wake's appointment, the School's Senior Field was the venue for the inspection of the Surrey Army Cadet Force. The visiting officer was the most famous living British soldier, Field Marshal Viscount Montgomery of Alamein. After inspecting the cadets he announced he wanted to know more about the School upon whose soil he trod. Thus began a relationship which was to span nearly thirty years. But before the impact upon the School of the Field Marshal is examined, it might be the moment to look back and take a glimpse at the quality of life of the boys and their teachers between the wars and during the Second World War.

First, to dispose of the years when there was no St. John's School, Leatherhead! At Speech Day in 1931 Edmund Downes made the curious announcement that henceforth the School was to be termed simply

'Leatherhead School'. He emphasised that the term 'Johnian' would still apply to old boys and to the magazine, but otherwise all references to the evangelist would cease. 'But there would always be "Johnians"' he concluded to thunderous applause. The term 'Leatherhead School' was duly used on all occasions for about seven years. By the outbreak of the Second World War 'St. John's School, Leatherhead' had reasserted itself – the fate of its nomenclature keeping pace with the state of its finances. There can be no certainty why this change occurred. There had always been some debate about the rather long-winded name of the School – as there was about the spelling of 'Leatherhead'. The town's name has nothing to do with the material made from animal skins and was originally spelt 'Letherhead'. When the school first moved to the town it was referred to as 'St. John's School, Letherhead' on much documentation. Purists were persistent in their denunciation of the decision to incorrectly impose the 'a'. What might explain the short-lived experiment of 'Leatherhead School' was the fact that in 1931 Downes was establishing his grand scheme of preparatory school foundationships. Indeed at the same Speech Day where he had announced the name change, the Archbishop of Canterbury, Cosmo Lang, made a resounding pledge of support for the Downes scheme. It might have been pressure from the preparatory schools, over sixty of them, many of them hitherto unknown to the School and scattered throughout the country, which pushed for a change.

Between the wars the School continued to build upon the academic successes of the Rutty years. External examinations in the form of School and Higher Certificates were undertaken by most pupils with gratifying success. Internal examinations were rigorous and most notorious of all were the 'viva voce' examinations conducted by Edmund Downes, continuing a tradition begun by Arthur Rutty. The Headmaster wandered around the school and every boy had to stand up before him and recite a piece of Latin prose or verse. If a boy did not do well the Headmaster would recommend to his Housemaster severe punishment, sometimes a caning. Philip Shenton remembered: 'Greatly feared were these examinations and many boys tried to escape them by shamming illness.' The School received a Board of Education Inspection in 1931 when five gentlemen appeared for four days and visited many classes. 'The Johnian' did not take the visit seriously; 'as an entertainment for the school the Inspection had its merits' was its dismissive comment. In fact, the Inspection had more impact than the writers of 'The Johnian' realised and led to the reprimanding of several teachers and the enforced retirement of one very long-serving member of the Common Room. (These Inspections were scheduled to occur only once every ten years).

Jack Carter's appointment in 1933 had heralded a period of improved teaching provision. He had been horrified by the absence of adequate science teaching facilities and the four new laboratories incorporated into the classroom block put the School's science facilities on a par with some of the best schools in the land. But 'science' before the war meant Physics and Chemistry – there was no specific Biology teaching at the school till 1945 when a Biology laboratory was extensively equipped thanks to a generous donation from the widow of a former Chairman of the Council, Francis Hopkins.

Most of the teaching staff were bachelors – and all the Housemasters were. The prospect of marriage meant a reconsideration of a career. 'Mr. Shanks' marriage has entailed his resignation from the West House tutor-ship,' Jack Carter informed the Council in 1937. Similar statements appear throughout the 1920s and 1930s. In 1943, Mr. Gettins, the first Housemaster of Churchill, left the School as a consequence of getting married. The provision of staff accommodation in the main building – and in Blocks A and B – precluded anything but the most basic of bachelor flats. It was Jack Carter, the only bachelor Headmaster, who did something about the marginalised married man by buying and building a number of family houses around the School estate. But even after this investment the pastoral side of the School was largely the responsibility of the bachelor master. After 1948, with the creation of Surrey House for day boys and then a larger increase in their numbers, married men were appointed to day housemasterships.

While Jack Carter was keen to create a school less dominated by the single man he remained a traditionalist in his belief in the all-round schoolmaster. A useful games player himself who had narrowly missed a rugby blue, he expected all the staff to participate fully in games. In 1938 he persuaded the Council to pay an extra increment to all staff with 'a distinguished athletic record.' The School continued to play competitive sport to a high level often against much larger schools. The 1942 1st XV went through the season unbeaten – and lost only one game the following season. P.W. Sykes won a cap for England in 1948 and J.H. Burges for Ireland in 1950.

Clubs and societies flourished in the School, particularly in the 1930s, and the Second World War, unlike the First, did not have a negative impact on the vitality of the school community. History, Natural History, Debating, Photography, Radio, Mountaineering, Geography, Gramophone, Shakespearian were all names of societies flourishing at the School. In addition there were lantern slide presentations, debates, mock trials and elections. In the 1931 mock election the Labour candidate, for the first and only time in St. John's history, won (this was the year the Labour Party were electorally destroyed as a consequence of the Depression). The Radio Club conducted two particularly enterprising projects outside their weekly meetings – in 1926 during the General Strike they picked up the BBC radio bulletins and transformed them into news sheets, distributing them around the School. (One pedantic master returned his with the spelling corrected). In 1936 the Club rigged up a radio system in the Chapel and relayed to the School the commentary on the funeral of George V.

From 1925 a small number of senior boys attended the Duke of York camps. These were summer camps for public schoolboys and youths from less privileged backgrounds. In the summer holiday the whole group – four hundred in number – would meet at Buckingham Palace and travel by train to New Romney where they would remain under canvas for a fortnight. The camps were the inspiration of the Duke of York – the future George VI – and he personally attended every one. The handful of senior Johnians who attended each year spoke with enthusiasm about the experience.

In 1924 the St. John's Mission was established at Walworth in South London. The Mission was the inspiration of Nathaniel Edwards, the incumbent of St. John's, Walworth. In fact the School had established links with a number of London parishes after the Great War – including

Walworth – and some senior boys and Old Boys were involved in a number of projects. But it was the dynamic and inspirational presence of Nathaniel Edwards which turned the St. John's Mission into something special. Tales of Father Edwards still circulate in the parish of Walworth where he was – and is – considered a saint. The most famous anecdote concerned his visit to a very poor family in the parish at the height of the Depression. The father of the household had a job interview the following day but, desperate for work though he was, could not attend because he could not afford to buy appropriate clothing. Father Edwards removed his clothes, gave them to the man and wandered home in his underwear.

Gathered around Nathaniel Edwards was a group of very committed Old Johnians many of whom were later to take Holy Orders. Together with the School prefects they ran the School side of the Mission. There were two set pieces to the Mission – the Summer Camp and the Whit Monday visit to Leatherhead. The Summer Camp ran for a fortnight in the middle of the summer holidays and usually took place at Cuckmere Haven on the Sussex coast (the alternative location was Aldeburgh in Suffolk). Those who participated in the camps were mainly the young-sters of the parish of St. John's, Walworth who were organised in three groups – those eighteen and over, those between fourteen and eighteen, and juniors aged twelve or thirteen. The camp was run by Nathaniel Edwards and his group of Old Johnians and School prefects. A number of parishioners helped with arrangements, including Mr. Rolfe, the one-legged verger of St. John's, Walworth whose presence – and culinary skills – lived long in the memory of Johnians. There was a strong religious element in the Camps – Mass was conducted by Father Edwards each day. Indeed, a notable aspect of the link with the parish of Walworth was that it provided Johnians with access to a more exotic brand of Anglicanism than they were accustomed to. Walworth's religion was of a higher altitude than Leatherhead's.

The Whit Monday visit to the School was a most elaborate occasion. Three hundred Walworth parishioners would descend upon the School for the day. The Headmaster and his wife would take the senior members of the parish on a motor trip around the North Downs while everyone else would be involved in a series of competitions with the boys. The School tended to win the cricket matches while Walworth won the boxing – though on one occasion the Walworth lads did beat the 1st XI, much to the embarrassment of the School cricket coach. The day concluded with an entertainment in Big School – play readings, songs, recitals – followed by a short religious service.

The Mission continued till 1960 but a combination of factors led to its dwindling support after the late 1930s. Nathaniel Edwards died in 1935 at the age of 57, worn out by his constant endeavours on behalf of his parishioners. There had always been a problem in involving more than a handful of members of the School on occasions other than the Whit Monday visits (although the choir gave an annual recital at Walworth). Every year Fr. Edwards would come to Leatherhead to promote the cause but a busy school life gave few opportunities for senior schoolboy involvement in Central London. The Mission was essentially the work of a handful of Old Boys, backed by a resolute body of senior boys, presided over by the charismatic presence of an obviously great man whose death took away much of the stimulus. There was also a changing attitude. Certainly by the 1940s – notably after the seismic shock of the 1945 election – public school 'missions' were seen as deeply patronising. The fact that the Mission continued till 1960 says much for its founder. A memorial to Nathaniel Edwards stands in the beautiful church of St. John's, Walworth. Anyone keen to pay respect to a great Johnian would do well to take the five minute walk to Larcom Street from the bustle of the Elephant and Castle.

There was another Edwards, infinitely less distinguished, who lived long in the memory of many Johnians. This was Jimmy Edwards – an eccentric down-and-out who lived in a makeshift shelter at the top of the Junior Field. Jimmy Edwards was extremely well spoken and his tales of coming from a propertied family were evidently true. What disaster had befallen the poor man was never made clear although he tended to blame the School, proclaiming to all boys who came across him that he had had land stolen from him by the School authorities. He wore eccentric attire – a dishevelled tailcoat and filthy striped trousers – and occasionally completed this formal dress with a bow tie. The kinder boys took a genuine interest in him while the more cruel found him an easy target for ridicule. The School Governors certainly did not find Jimmy Edwards amusing as they were constantly harassed by a stream of letters complaining that they had not paid him for his land. This appeared to refer to the four acres of land west of the Senior Field purchased in 1912. On one occasion Jimmy Edwards arranged for a large mound of earth to be dumped at the entry to the Senior Field, thus preventing entry. It took several days for the School authorities to have it moved. Jimmy Edwards was a notable character around the School and many Old Boys had clear memories of him. He was found dead in his hut in 1925 and there was a lengthy obituary of him in 'The Johnian'.

Although the quality of life of the boys was spartan by the standards of the new millennium, in one area they had an advantage over the contemporary Johnian. They were serviced by large numbers of servants. There was virtually no general fagging for menial tasks were undertaken by a regiment of 'skivvies'. There was personal fagging – prefects and members of the 1st XV and 1st XI were entitled to a personal fag – but cleaning chores, serving food and the early morning wake-up call were all the duties of the servants. The food was poor, particularly in the 1920s. Breakfast comprised porridge or bread and margarine; lunch was meat and stodgy pudding – with boiled fish on a Friday; one particularly unpopular pudding was termed an 'Olaf' for some unknown reason. There was a late afternoon tea of bread and margarine and, finally, supper (termed 'dogger') comprising a large biscuit. It was the custom to avoid this final meal of the day – indeed anyone partaking of this biscuit tended to be mocked by his colleagues: many a small boy went hungry to bed rather than face the ridicule of his friends.

The most frequent form of punishment was the detention. This was given for a variety of offences and came in four time segments; half-an-hour, one hour, one-and-a-half hours and two hours. For a serious offence a beating was followed by a two-hour detention. A detention involved walking round and round the Gymnasium under the supervision of the School Sergeant – for many years, Sergeant Whelan. 'It was boring in the extreme', remembered one Old Boy, 'and only enlivened by the rude two-finger signs made by some of the marchers'. Indeed, the

School Sergeant did not appear to have the discipline that the Headmaster and the Housemasters might have wished: apart from being subjected to rude signs from some malcontents he failed to notice the absence of many of his charges. It was common practice for those boys with long detentions to slip away for a while and return for the final few circuits.

The General Strike in 1926 made a large impact on the School with several masters signing up to assist the government. 'The masters seemed to have joined the Special Constabulary in a body,' reported 'The Johnian', 'some mounting guard over a petrol pump and others peacefully playing rummy in a first class carriage in the railway sidings. Much to the disappointment of the forms concerned they appeared promptly at nine the next morning as if they had slept all night.' One boy commented on the problems of taking the bus to Epsom during the General Strike: the buses had volunteers as both drivers and conductors – the conductors took no notice of official fares and either charged nothing at all or made up a grossly inflated fare. Most boys, like the staff, were totally supportive of the government but a few rebellious spirits did defend the strikers – they did not impress the editors of 'The Johnian': 'The Red Flag, that most dismal of ditties, was sung by loungers in the alcove,' was the dismissive comment on these class traitors.

The period between the wars saw a thankful lessening of the illnesses and epidemics which had been such a hallmark of the School up until 1919. Measles, mumps, influenza and scarlet fever continued to hit the School regularly but not with the impact of the earlier decades. There were still some tragedies. In a three-week period in 1936, two boys died at the School: Oscar Elkington aged 17 and Arthur Wardell aged 12. Oscar died of a heart attack in the middle of the 1st XV match against Cranleigh. Amazingly the game continued and the report of the match in 'The Johnian' made no reference to the tragedy. Arthur, who had a history of heart problems, collapsed on getting out of the swimming bath just after a House swimming session.

When boys needed to be taken to hospital in Epsom use was sometimes made of Mr. Still, Chairman of the Council between 1918 and 1930, who lived at 'Windfield', opposite the school. His large chauffeur-driven car was used to transport the boys to hospital in some style.

The ominous political events of the late 1930s were recorded in 'The Johnian' and, along with most of the country, there was considerable rejoicing in the School at Neville Chamberlain's deal struck with Hitler in Munich in 1938. The sense of relief was palpable – it brought to an end, briefly, a long period of preparation for war. 'We emerged from the crisis with a satisfactory feeling that in the event of a future emergency we would be fully prepared. The basements were rendered gas-proof, their windows were covered in cellophane paper or wire-netting to guard against splintering; vulnerable windows were protected by ramparts of earth or sandbags; gas masks were fitted and issued to the school and staff and air-raid practices were carried out to test our emergency routine.' The relief, of course, was shortlived and little more than twenty years after the end of the First World War the School had to face another conflict. Eighty-eight Johnians were to die in the Second World War, a little more than half the number which died in the earlier conflagration. But the depth of tragedy cannot be measured by the numbers of lives lost. There were particularly poignant incidents. The old Headmaster, Edmund Downes, lost two of his three sons. The young priest, Vivian Redlich, performing missionary work in Papua New Guinea, was cut down by the Japanese when he refused to leave his village. He is now proclaimed an Anglican martyr. In the First World War the first officer to be killed in combat was a Johnian, two days after the outbreak of the War. In 1939, in similar circumstances, another Johnian, Lt. David Williams, was killed when his ship, HMS Courageous, was torpedoed on September 17 1939 – two weeks after the outbreak of war.

There were moments of pride. Lt. Colonel Derek Seagrim of the Green Howards was awarded a posthumous VC for his conduct on the Mareth Line in Tunisia in March 1943. His actions were described in the London Gazette: 'From the time the attack was launched his battalion was subjected to the most intense fire from artillery, machine guns and mortars. Realising the seriousness of the situation, Lt. Col. Seagrim placed himself at the head of his battalion and led it through a hail of fire. He personally helped the team which was placing the scaling ladder over the anti-tank ditch and was himself the first to cross it. He led the assault firing his pistol, throwing grenades and personally assaulting two machine gun posts. It is estimated that in this phase he killed or captured 20 Germans. This display of personal courage led directly to the capture of the objective. By his valour, disregard for personal safety and outstanding example he so inspired his men that the battalion success-fully took and held its objective, thereby allowing the attack to proceed. Lt. Col. Seagrim subsequently died of wounds received in action.'

There were light-hearted moments too – often provided by the new Bursar, the Old Johnian Billy Rivers, who bought a house close to the School and offered his services free of charge. The 'real' Bursar, Mr. Rainier, was called up for war service, so the Council leapt at the oppor-tunity of a free Bursar. Billy and Judy Rivers had recently returned from Burma where they had managed a vast plantation. With Mr. Gray, who had come up from the London office in 1935, seeing to all routine admin-istration, Billy and Judy Rivers were to involve themselves fully in the community of the School. A warm working and social relationship was struck with the Headmaster. It was a typical gesture of warmth and friendship that led the Headmaster and the Bursar to offer facilities at St. John's to the 150 girls of St. Martins-in-the-Field School for Girls who had been forced from their premises in Tulse Hill, South London. The girls were lodged in and around Leatherhead from October 1939 and at first their only schoolroom was the Methodist Hall. Jack Carter and Billy Rivers offered the classrooms and games fields at St. John's and a fee of £1 a term per pupil was agreed. The Council spent the rest of the war trying to get a larger payment from the Governors of St. Martins, claiming the girls were making far more use of St. John's than was intended. Indeed the whole episode does have a flavour of the popular play of the 1950s, 'The Happiest Days of Your Life'. A system operated where the girls used the classrooms while the boys were on the games fields and the girls played their sports while the boys were in class. This neat sexual segregation broke down when boys found feminine items in the drawers of the desks or came across a girl's hat hanging on their coat peg.

'We have been discreetly invaded by St. Martins-in-the-Field Girls School', moaned 'The Johnian'. Every effort was made to prevent the two communities meeting but inevitably one or two romantic relation-ships did develop. The boys received the distinct impression that the whole exercise met with disapproval from the St. John's teaching staff, which was perhaps a little less fun-loving than before, now its younger element had gone off to fight.

Apart from the girls of St. Martins the impact of the War on the community of the School was not marked – not nearly as dramatic as the impact of the First World War. A quarter of the teaching staff went off to fight and retired schoolmasters and a few ladies were recruited to fill the gap. Rationing and black-outs obviously made an impact and in 1941 the School suffered extensive physical damage when two mines were dropped on the Gymnasium. But societies and sports continued; indeed the war years were particularly impressive ones for school teams. As in the First War, the cadet force came into its own with duties performed around the town and increased numbers of exercises in the school grounds and on Headley Common.

'The Johnian' magazine was by now appearing termly. The Lent Term 1945 edition appeared in March while Russian tanks were rumbling on the outskirts of Berlin. 'We timidly wonder', wrote the editor, 'we dare to hope that perhaps the next Johnian will be written in an atmosphere of peace.' The next 'Johnian' did appear in July 1945 with the War in Europe over but it was not until August 1945 that the School could begin to function once more in a country at peace.

CHAPTER TEN

The Field Marshal:
The significance of
Viscount Montgomery of Alamein
1948–1966

HEREWARD WAKE HAD BEEN HEADMASTER FOR A YEAR when a fortuitous moment on the Senior Field brought into the midst of the School a legendary figure who was to make an enormous contribution, personally and financially, to the well-being of the community. The most obvious monument to the work of Field Marshal Lord Montgomery was the new School Chapel, erected in 1962, but in many other areas of the School, and in the lives of many pupils, staff and governors, his mark has been left.

Hereward Wake, a descendant of the great Anglo-Saxon patriot and scourge of the Normans, came to St. John's from the same school as his predecessor, Cheltenham College. He was forty-eight when he became Headmaster, a year older than Jack Carter. He was married with two sons and had been educated at Marlborough and Keble College, Oxford; a fine rugby player he had won a 'blue' in 1922 and went on to captain Somerset in 1927. He took over the School at a moment of optimism when numbers were high and with the School once again showing its commitment to the clergy as well as attracting full fee-paying pupils. When he retired in 1960 the School had 350 pupils – an increase in numbers of fifteen per cent; but what was of most significance was the make-up of the pupil population: over 200 were non-clergy children and there was a large Sixth Form of 130. There had been an opportunity to take in even more non-Foundationers by increasing the numbers of day boys but a policy was decided to keep these at about 60 in number. While not undervaluing the quiet and competent skills of the Headmaster during the 1950s, there is no question that in these years the key figure associated with the administration of the School was the awe-inspiring, difficult, far from humble victor of El Alamein.

Monty was to recall his first contact with St. John's. 'I first came into contact with the school by mere chance. I was inspecting a parade of Surrey cadets on the school cricket ground. The boys were all looking on as spectators and I went over to see them. I liked the look of them and made enquiries about the school.'

Hereward Wake arranged for the Field Marshal to be given a tour of the School. He was asked to present the prizes at the forthcoming Speech Day and some months later was invited to join the School Council. There was more than a touch of self-interest behind the invitation of the Council. The centenary of the School was approaching and thought was being given as to how this might be celebrated. To have on the governing body a household name, someone with a huge network of highly-placed contacts and who possessed unrivalled skills of self-promotion could only be an asset. The Field Marshal accepted the invitation though he did inform the Chairman, Sir George Lloyd Jacob, that his extensive commitments would undoubtedly mean irregular attendance at meetings. (In fact Monty's attendance record was exemplary – something Sir George Lloyd Jacob would regret.) For a year the Field Marshal took a back seat – as far as such a man could ever take a back seat – and attended meetings as often as his busy schedule would permit. He had just become a governor of his old school, St. Paul's, at a time when his political and military responsibilities were awesome. Monty had been Chief of the Imperial General Staff between 1946 and 1948 when he became Chairman of the Western Union commanders-in-chief (the Western Union was a defensive alliance of European states which predated the formation of NATO); this post involved his spending considerable periods of time at his French headquarters outside Paris, Château de Courances.

In 1950 the Governors of the School invited Monty to be Chairman of the Council for the following year, the year of the centenary celebrations. The idea was that Sir George Lloyd Jacob would step down for one year only to enable Monty to be chairman during all the activities surrounding the centenary celebrations. This seemed a fair and sensible course of action in recognition of the fact that Monty was already in contact with characters as different as J. Arthur Rank, the film mogul, and Mrs. Attlee, the Prime Minister's wife, to promote the cause of the School. There was some doubt as to whether Monty would be able to take on the one-year appointment. But he agreed to – and was still Chairman sixteen years later (to the dismay of Sir George Lloyd Jacob).

Monty's tenure of office as Chairman of the Council was a period of immense activity which began with the events surrounding the centenary. A Centenary Appeal was established which raised £35,000. A splendid dinner was held at the Mansion House where the guests of honour were the Duke and Duchess of Gloucester. The royal premiere of the Ealing Comedy, 'The Lavender Hill Mob', was performed at the Odeon, Marble Arch, with the proceeds going to the School. It was fortunate – and somewhat typical of Monty's touch – that the film was a huge commercial and critical success and the School was able to bask in a little of its glory. There was no questioning the events of the Centenary had been a triumph; only the bravest of souls would want to remind Monty of his agreement to stand down from the chairmanship at the end of 1951. For half of the period of Monty's chairmanship – till 1958 – he was overseeing the affairs of the School while holding down key political and military appointments in Europe, as well as creating considerable controversy with his frequent critical remarks, invariably aimed at the Americans, about the conduct of the war. In 1958, at the age of 71, he retired as Deputy Supreme Commander of NATO and was able to devote even more time to the affairs of the School. In an interview in 'The Sunday Times' at the time of his retirement, Monty was asked how he intended spending his time. 'Working for and helping youth', he replied, 'not by prize-giving ceremonies but by spending a couple of nights at a school or a gathering of apprentices and debating with them the situation in the world.'

If the picture being created is the familiar one of Monty, the egomaniac anxious to find any new stage upon which to strut, then this needs to be balanced by referring to his endless acts of personal generosity towards the School, most of which attracted no publicity and went unheralded other than by the gratitude of the recipients. In 1956 an Industrial Fund Committee was established where British industrialists contributed sums of money to enable independent schools to re-equip their science laboratories: to receive benefit from the Fund a school had to contribute one-third of the cost itself and then the Fund would pay the remaining two-thirds. St. John's was keen to take the opportunity to update its science teaching facilities but faced problems finding the £5,000 which would represent the School's contribution. Monty made a personal gift of the money – so the School received £10,000 from the Industrial Fund Committee. In 1958 Monty provided a further £5,000 to help fund a series of improvements to the School's amenities, including the 'rejuvenation' of the Chapel organ. In 1959 he bought a TV for the Sixth Form and funded the re-equipment of the sanatorium. In 1964 he funded the provision of a twenty-four booth language laboratory and a year later paid for the redecoration of the Dining Hall. On top of this material generosity Monty was diligent in his promotion of the School – recommending it to parents and explaining its purpose and mission whenever he had the opportunity. He committed all his earnings from newspaper articles and book reviews to the School. His most palpable act of support for the School was the encouragement he gave to the construction of the new Chapel. By 1960 the old Chapel was too small to accommodate the whole school so there was a pressing need for a larger building. The estimated cost, however, was £50,000 which was a sum of money the School would find difficulty raising (in fact it was a sum of money amounting to the size of the School overdraft in 1960.) At a Council meeting Monty announced that he had found an anonymous donor to provide the sum of money – and duly £50,000 was handed over to the School and promptly invested in the Chapel building account. The anonymous donor was never revealed.

Perhaps the best illustration of Monty's feeling for the School, though, was not seen in sums of money or bricks and mortar but through the experience of four Sixth Formers on a cycling holiday in France in the summer vacation of 1952. Monty had met them at a School function and told them to look in at Château de Courances should they be cycling past. Nigel Hamilton, Monty's biographer, described Courances as a 'seventeenth century palace with an elegant, double-carved staircase rising to the front doors' and 'formal gardens, waterworks and woods.'[1] Monty, naturally, loved living and working in such opulent surroundings but four Johnian cyclists staring up the drive on a hot August afternoon had their misgivings. They did, however, decide to take up the invitation and cycled up to the grand entrance announcing they were guests of the Field Marshal. They were provided with lavish bedrooms, access to baths and showers, and a fine dinner. They were shown the grand billiard room and in the evening Monty appeared, after a hard day supervising NATO, and played billiards with the boys – who were impressed by his skill. The following day they cycled off to continue their vacation in less sumptuous surroundings.

Monty's chairmanship of the Council, though, was more than a tale of largesse and publicity. Sharp debates were conducted in Council meetings about the future direction of the School. These debates were the consequence of the changing circumstances in which the School was operating as well as Monty's very clear ideas about the future of St. John's.

At the end of the Second World War the McNair Committee on teachers' pay recommended substantial increases in the payment for teachers and stated their salaries and conditions of employment should be equated with those of the administrative and executive branches of the Civil Service. The Burnham Committee, which oversaw teachers' pay, subsequently took these recommendations into account and provided a new scale with large increases for teachers and – significantly for independent boarding schools – the provision of extra allowances for special duties: the proposal provoked discussion at St. John's in both common room and Council meetings. The Headmaster was able to report to the Council in 1951: 'It was the unanimous conclusion of the staff that the nomination of selected masters as holders of posts of special responsibility should not be instituted at St. John's.' He went on, 'This conclusion reflects the team spirit of the whole staff and should not be

---

[1] Hamilton, N., *Monty: The Field Marshal, 1944–1976.*

applied to their financial detriment.' The Council took the point – the teachers at St. John's would be performing duties at the School which would have been rewarded in the state sector with extra allowances. It was important, therefore, that this be recognised with a pay scale more generous than the Burnham Scale. The School committed itself to paying above Burnham by two increments in recognition of the tasks expected of the teachers outside the classroom. This was a major commitment which would rest heavily on the School's finances.

At the same time, in 1951, there was a further visit from the schools' inspectors. While the report of the inspectors was mainly encouraging, a number of serious problems were highlighted. The Field Marshal was keen for action to be taken on several recommendations. Reference was made to 'undue pressure on existing staff', and the Headmaster was requested to explain what this problem was and how it might be resolved. The inspectors took issue with the fact that no timetable concessions were made for any positions of responsibility – Housemasters, for example, had a full teaching commitment and their pastoral role was loaded on to the classroom programme. 'Pressure', answered Hereward Wake, 'is cheerfully borne by the staff and I can detect none of the Trade Union attitude towards conditions of service that has been in evidence in certain other quarters of the teaching profession.' Both the Headmaster and the Council were reluctant to employ more teaching staff particularly now that they had made the employment of teachers a relatively expensive business. Nevertheless the comments of the inspectors had to be acted upon – reference, for example, was made to the teaching of Art which was 'taught by a man who at the same time is a Housemaster, Head of the Modern Languages department and Careers Master.' Eventually a part-time Biology teacher and a part-time Art teacher were appointed to offer some relief to the full-time staff.

Another criticism made by the inspectors was the quality of the dayrooms in the School and the numbers of baths. Monty was in total agreement about this and was determined to improve the living and recreational facilities in the school. 'The dayrooms are a disgrace', he proclaimed at a Council meeting. He set in motion a programme of improvement, funded largely from the Centenary Appeal Fund but with frequent contributions from himself. The whole issue of what the School should be spending money on however, threw open once more the debate over what the School was really about – with one of the participants in the debate being the acerbic and vitriolic Field Marshal it was inevitable there were going to be moments of heat in the meetings of the Council. Monty's agenda was straightforward: a commitment to the sons of the clergy, certainly, but only to take in the number which could be afforded; every effort must be made to make the School attractive to full fee-paying parents because, given the commitment to a modern salary structure for staff and better conditions for pupils, increasing fee income was the pre-requisite for everything else. 'I consider it unsound to go on living from hand to mouth and just managing to make ends meet,' he told the Council.

Sir George Lloyd Jacob, the former Chairman of the Council and now Vice-Chairman, had the temerity to question Monty's priorities. He made his situation worse in the eyes of the Field Marshal when he suggested Monty's workload was too great for him to be an effective Chairman. 'In a letter to me the Vice-Chairman made it very clear that in his view I cannot adequately carry out the duties of Chairman because of my many commitments.' The dispute between the two men was a clash of personalities, some resentment on the part of Sir George that he had not returned to the chairmanship as originally agreed, but, more importantly, it was a conflict about the future of the School. Monty wrote to the Council: 'I am under the impression he considers we are spending too much. He considers the money collected in the Centenary Year should be spent firstly on maintaining the present level of Foundationers. He considers I am persuading the Council to spend too much money on improving the physical conditions of the school to the detriment of the Foundation.'

Monty won the dispute but it is noticeable that this debate, a century old, should be more heated than ever in the 1950s. Sir George lay low on the Council for a year or so before once more taking up regular attendance. He did not resign till 1965, a year before Monty, by which time their differences were resolved. Monty, in fact, managed to take the issue of the Foundation a stage further by 'taking a full and bold decision to

The modern classroom extension was opened in 1998 by the Duchess of Gloucester; its architecture is in keeping with the buildings of 'The Quad'.

Girls arrived at St. John's in 1989 and quickly made their mark. This is the successful lacrosse team of 1991.

The manly sports continue. The successful Rugby Sevens team who won the Worth Shield Competition, 2001.

The new Chapel was largely funded by an anonymous donor arranged by
Field Marshal Montgomery. It was built in 1962 and continues to be a focal point
of School activities.

reduce the number of Foundationers down to, say, 140'. This figure was agreed. A ceiling of 140 was put on the number of clergy children in the School while the number of non-clergy continued to expand.

Indeed the number of pupils at the School expanded throughout the late 1950s and into the early 1960s. In 1957 Hereward Wake increased the Common Entrance pass mark to 65% for day boys and 60% for boarders. In 1958 he was able to tell the Council: 'In 1948 twenty boys obtained their Higher Certificates; in 1958 seventy-eight boys took the equivalent examinations.... . This term we have 130 boys in the VI form.' So many boys were entering the school that they could not all be accommodated in the main buildings. One of the masters, Mr. Tait, began a 'Waiting House' in Linden Gardens where he and his wife supervised up to twenty boys waiting to go into the main school. More property was bought for married staff – another policy much supported by Monty. In 1950 a member of the Council, a former president of the Law Society, Sir Alan Gillett, sold his house 'Hallaton' to the School for £5,500; the School eventually turned it into three staff flats before it became the girls' House in 1989.

In 1960 Hereward Wake retired to Chichester after twelve years as Headmaster. The period had been one of growth and consolidation. His calm and amiable presence had been a needed contrast to the bombastic brilliance of the Field Marshal. Monty now took a personal interest in finding a new Headmaster for 'my school'. He was found teaching Classics at Harrow – a 33-year-old first class honours graduate from Sidney Sussex College, Cambridge, who had begun his teaching career at Christ's Hospital before moving to Harrow in 1952. Ian Sutherland was to be the Headmaster for exactly a decade – the significant decade of the 1960s. For little over half this period Monty continued to dominate the proceedings of the Council. He made frequent visits to the School, continued to give generously to a variety of School projects, and entertained the staff to an annual dinner at the House of Lords. He eventually retired in 1966 as his eightieth birthday loomed before him.

Why did the Field Marshal become so involved in the School ? It is a question often asked and only a speculative answer can be given. He was, of course, the son of a clergyman himself so the notion of a school for the sons of the clergy would have found favour. He was also a deeply religious man with a faith which was robust and straightforward. 'The Church must tell the soldiers not what is, but what should be behind their going forth,' he stated in the middle of the Second World War. More famously he also stated, 'I would as soon think of going into battle without my artillery as without my Chaplain.' It is important not to enter the realm of amateur psychiatry but it is recognised that Monty was a lonely man – a widower with a dislocated domestic and family life. He thrived in institutions and the institution became the family where he had a role. St. John's became a replacement regiment with the Field Marshal commanding from the front. Monty also had a genuine interest in young people – there are many examples of his giving up much of his time to be with them: from the young Swiss boy, Lucien Treub, he befriended just after the War to the cast of 'Oliver' whom he entertained for the day at his Hampshire home, Isington Mill, in 1964. He was happy in the company of the young. When he died in 1976, at his request, a contingent from the St. John's School Cadet Force helped line the procession route for his state funeral at Windsor. It had indeed been a happy day for the School when, in 1948, he had wandered across the Senior Field to talk to – and be so impressed with – a group of young Johnians.

CHAPTER ELEVEN

Challenges and Changes: The School since the 1970s

IAN SUTHERLAND WAS STILL IN HIS EARLY FORTIES WHEN he resigned as headmaster in 1970. He became Director of Education and Training for the Heath Education Council and continued there till his retirement. He died aged 73 in 1999. The 1960s had been an uneasy decade in which to direct the fortunes of a public school. The educational reforms of the late 1960s brought an end to direct grant schools and the entry into the private sector of academically strong day schools providing tough – and relatively cheap – competition to the established independent sector. Increasing fees meant parents found greater difficulty in funding private education and consequently became more discerning in their choice of school. With St. John's there was the specific issue of the Foundation; soaring costs meant the funds of the Foundation covered the costs of fewer clergy children. It was important that these pupils were not educated at a loss nor that their education was subsidised by the fees of the non-clergy parent. Yet reduced numbers of clergy boys would mean empty beds in boarding Houses unless there was an increased number of non-clergy boarders, which was unlikely while traditional boarding slipped out of fashion. Preparatory schools found it more difficult to offer the generous terms to the clergy negotiated by Edmund Downes thirty years earlier and one by one they left the scheme. On top of all this there was the culture of the 1960s. Its wilder excesses made little impact in Epsom Road but there was evidence of some student unrest. Objections were raised about compulsion: to be compelled to do anything in the 1960s was likely to provoke hostility. Complaints were made about compulsory Chapel and a compulsory cadet force. Discontent, though, did not develop beyond arguments, petitions or provocatively long hair. More serious, perhaps, for the Headmaster was staff unease after 1964. In that year three members of staff were asked to relinquish their posts. At a time when redundancies were unheard of in the tranquil waters of public school employment, their enforced resignations caused a stir. All three were clergymen and the authorities felt the School could not sustain three clerics simultaneously in the Common Room. Whatever the arguments for or against the action there is no doubt that it led to considerable Common Room tension at a time when the School was facing a struggle to maintain its numbers. The Headmaster, too, was dealing with a new generation of Housemasters. (Hereward Wake had instigated the 'fifteen-year rule' – still applicable – where Housemasters relinquished their posts after a maximum of fifteen years; he considered it important that holders of senior posts had a break after a lengthy period in office; he also believed the boys would benefit from a change of regime; he wanted, too, to have more flexibility in 'middle management' posts in order to provide promotion opportunities for ambitious teachers). So, in the early 1960s the generation of Housemasters appointed after the war gave way to a new group, several of whom were to continue into the 1980s. Ian Sutherland also had to contend with the continued presence of the Field Marshal. While Monty had retired as Chairman of the Council in 1966, he had been made honorary President and continued to voice his strong feelings on matters pertaining to the governance of the School. In 1969, for example, he expressed his disapproval of the proposed appeal believing this was no longer an appropriate manner of raising funds for the School. (In fact an appeal was launched which funded several of the projects of the new Headmaster, Ted Hartwell).

The largest problem for the School in the 1960s, however, was the perennial issue of its constituency: its total number and the make-up of that total number. In 1970 there were 340 pupils in the School of whom just 60 were day boys – mostly residing in the single day House, Surrey. There were 100 Foundationers, all of whom were boarders. These numbers showed little movement – indeed a small decline – from Hereward Wake's period.

The new Headmaster, Ted Hartwell, set in motion a strategy which was to shape the character of the school for the future and which essentially remains intact today. While maintaining a commitment to its charitable Foundation, the School would educate clergy sons only in numbers which it could afford to sustain through its donations; while continuing to operate as a boarding school there would be an energetic policy of attracting more day pupils and, for the longer term, the new Headmaster raised the issue of co-education.

Before Ted Hartwell's arrival – from Charterhouse – the School's attitude to day pupils had been wary. There had always been some day boys at the School but they were never part of the Foundation; they were 'extras' who in the early years provided additional revenue for the Headmaster. Even in the 1950s there was hostility to the idea of building up the day boy community. When it was proposed that 'Windfield', the large house opposite the main school building, be used to house day boys, the idea was rejected on the grounds of expense and it was also made clear the School did not seek to encourage too many day pupils. This attitude might seem hard to comprehend. Leatherhead and its surrounding suburban enclave was ideal day boy country. Prosperous commuters with no interest in or tradition of boarding education constituted a strong potential market for a day school. Increasingly feeder preparatory schools were shedding their boarders. Yet there were problems. An excess of day boys might create a beleaguered boarding community. Day boys would rarely be sons of clergy so there might be an erosion still further of the community of Foundationers. An emphasis on day pupils might create a 'day boy mentality' in the Common Room with fewer staff being attracted to an involvement in boarding. In addition, the School would be entering a highly competitive market where academically prestigious schools were already well established. But, despite these reservations, it was clear to the new Headmaster that the School had little option but to move into the day boy market on a scale previously untried. It did so with huge success and within a decade the constituency of St. John's had been transformed.

With an influx of day boys, Surrey House could no longer remain as the single day House. In the early 1970s boarding in North House was phased out so that by 1975 it was an exclusively day House. In the vacant spaces of Block A – day Houses, of course, do not require the same extent of accommodation – a new day House was established, Montgomery. So by the middle of the 1970s there were three day Houses, Surrey, North and Montgomery, and three boarding Houses, South, East and West. Churchill House, sole occupant of Block B, began to take in day boys too but held on to its boarding community, thus becoming the only mixed House. In 2000 the School comprised 440 pupils – 280 of whom were day pupils and 160 were boarders.

Despite this transformation of the School community it remained structured on boarding school lines and, alongside the appeal to day pupils there were efforts to recruit more boarders. In the middle of the 1960s Ian Sutherland had first considered the option of weekly boarding where boys could return home on Saturday afternoons and come back to school on Sunday evenings. The proposal had been rejected on the grounds it would make full boarding even less attractive and there would be difficulties in sustaining Sunday morning worship. In the late 1980s the proposal was put forward again and this time met with a more sympathetic response. A compromise policy of fortnightly *exeats* was introduced; full weekly boarding followed a couple of years later. The timing of this was fortunate. In 1983 the M25 was extended beyond Leatherhead with a turn-off less than a mile from the School. Weekly boarding became an attractive proposition for those who in previous decades would have been unable to take advantage of it.

To maintain a sizeable boarding community the School, like most boarding schools, developed an overseas community. There had always been a few overseas pupils in the School but in the 1970s substantial numbers of boys from Hong Kong sought entry. More recently the international community has widened to include many nationalities including sizeable groups from South Korea and mainland China. It would be fair to say that initially the attraction of overseas students to the

School was their willingness to fill empty spaces in boarding Houses but recently a more positive and imaginative approach has been developed with a specialist teacher appointed to oversee the linguistic and pastoral development of students. In 2000 the overseas community comprised approximately seven per cent of the School population. Again, the location of the School was hugely beneficial in attracting overseas students. When one Housemaster enquired of a new pupil from Hong Kong what had drawn him to St. John's he was given a straightforward answer: keen to be told that the fame of the School had spread across the globe, the Housemaster was in fact informed that the boy's father, on examining a map of the British Isles, had calculated that St. John's was the one boarding school in the United Kingdom which was equidistant between Gatwick and Heathrow.

While the huge increase in the numbers of day boys altered many aspects of the School, in essence its ethos remained intact. A more radical change came in 1989 with the opening of Hallaton as the girls' House. This was the culmination of a debate that had been taking place for twenty years. The issue of co-education at St. John's had been controversial ever since it was first seriously proposed by Ted Hartwell in the early 1970s. As with many traditional boys' schools contemplating the move to co-education, the authorities had to give thought to motivation and consequences. Were girls being invited to join the School simply because empty spaces needed filling? Or was there a genuine belief that a co-educational community would be good for both girls and boys – and staff? If co-education was 'a good thing' then why restrict it to the Sixth Form? Was the intention to add girls to the School to make it larger, or to recruit them in place of boys, in which case there might be a weakening of traditional male pursuits like competitive rugby and cricket with a consequent loss of status in the eyes of the more traditionally inclined? There was also the issue of relations with the local girls' schools. It was clear that if the School were to become co-educational it would be recruiting girls from the local independent girls' schools which had already suffered as a consequence of several large boys' schools becoming co-educational. In the case of St. John's there was also the specific issue of the Foundation – the School was founded to provide an education for the sons of poor clergymen. The Charity Commission would need to approve so significant a change in the policy of the School.

Ted Hartwell's attempts to introduce a co-educational Sixth Form in the mid-1970s were frustrated because most members of the Council believed the disadvantages outweighed the advantages. In 1978, by way of compromise, an attempt was made to establish links with Parsons Mead School, a well-established girls' independent school just two miles away in Ashtead. Discussions were entered into which would have involved some form of amalgamation between the two schools. A decision was postponed because Parsons Mead was about to appoint a new Headmistress whose involvement was deemed crucial. The moment passed. But from the early 1980s it became increasingly clear that a co-educational Sixth Form at the School was inevitable and the new Headmaster in 1985, David Brown, was clearly in favour of progressing in that direction as quickly as possible.

In 1987 the Council voted in favour of establishing a co-educational Sixth Form and immediately a girls' sub-committee was established to oversee the practical implications of the decision. Soon after the Charity Commission gave its approval. Hallaton, the house in Garlands Road arranged as flats for married staff, would be the girls' House and £120,000 was spent converting it to its new purpose. The first Johnian girls – 21 of them – entered the School in September 1989. While they were based in Hallaton they were also attached to the boys' Houses – a decision which was changed in 1993 to enable Hallaton to have the same status and function as the traditional Houses. Whatever the earlier arguments about the wisdom of co-education there are few who would deny that the decision to take in girls has brought huge benefits to the School. In 2000 there were 45 girls in the School divided equally between day and boarding pupils.

The establishment of girls at St. John's, however, did not come at an auspicious moment. The late 1980s and early 1990s witnessed an economic recession which had serious consequences for all independent schools. The timing of the arrival of the girls might suggest a policy conjured up to fill empty spaces created by the recession – ignoring the fact that co-education was an issue which had been under review for many years. In the late 1980s the number of pupils at the School was higher than it had ever been but there was a worrying decline in parents registering for the School in the early 1990s. In addition there was a severe reduction in boarding numbers. By 1993, the traditional House structure had become untenable. Churchill House, the one established mixed House, had over eighty boys while the traditional boarding Houses, South, East and West, had under forty. It was clear too that boarding facilities in the School were not keeping pace with rivals. For some time there had been discussions about the rationalising of the boarding Houses – a sensitive topic because this obviously meant the closing down of one House with its members being dispersed into the others. When the concept of 'House spirit' was encouraged at every opportunity, to rip it away on grounds of rationalisation was bound to prompt dismay. But a difficult decision needed to be made. The new Headmaster, Christopher Tongue, decided to close down South House in 1993 and its members were placed into either East or West. This boosted the numbers in the remaining boarding Houses and created more spacious boarding facilities. The display of South House rugby shirts hung from the windows on the days following the decision was one indication that the demise of South did not go unmourned.

The recession had bitten hard into the School by the early 1990s and this prompted new strategies for increasing numbers. In 1992 Sir Douglas Lowe, a member of the Council, chaired a committee which considered a number of radical proposals aimed at rebuilding the School roll, which, already in decline, seemed set to fall considerably by the mid-1990s. While the majority of the committee favoured a series of radical measures, it was agreed that decisions should await the appointment of the new Headmaster – David Brown having resigned early in 1992.

The arrival of Christopher Tongue in January 1993 heralded a period of intense activity. With all the discussions which had taken place behind closed doors over the School's future the voice of the current parent was noticeably absent and a marketing survey was conducted to discover the feelings of those who had purchased a St. John's education. Similarly the views of preparatory school Headmasters were sought. At the same time many members of the staff were involved in a series of working parties to examine all aspects of the School's arrangements from the tutorial system to the practicalities of arranging coach transport from various parts of Surrey. The School uniform changed as well as the method of purchasing that uniform. A Student Council was established to provide an opportunity for the boys and girls to voice their opinions. At the end of the year there were excellent examination results to applaud. By the middle of the 1990s, with the recession coming to an end, the numbers entering the School once more began to rise. In 2000 there were almost one hundred more pupils in the School than there had been in 1993 – a period of expansion unparalleled since the time of Arthur Rutty a century earlier. The 1993 marketing survey had indicated broad satisfaction with the structure of the School while highlighting areas which needed improvement. There have been regular surveys of parental and preparatory school opinion ever since.

At stages in this history of St. John's there have been pauses in the narrative to consider the quality of life of the teachers and the taught. The changes to the quality of life, for better and for worse, have been so enormous in the past twenty-five years that a volume could be written on this topic alone. A single image might suffice to indicate change. Between the two World Wars a young Johnian might go to bed hungry – hunger being preferable to the humiliation of eating the disgusting final meal of the day, the 'dogger'. Today, of an evening, it is customary to see a motor scooter arrive at the front of the School carrying pizzas for those students feeling a little peckish (the delivery service having been summoned, of course, by mobile phone). There is a transformation in facilities with emphasis on the need for space and privacy. The colours system – the rewarding of achievement through the use of insignia – is no longer monopolised by sport; boys and girls are consulted on issues which affect them; potential School prefects apply for their posts and produce their curricula vitae prior to an interview; there is no longer fagging – even the harmless 'fagging lobbies' containing toasters and kettles had to change their nomenclature for fear of provoking images of a bygone age. Changes for residential staff might have been a little less dramatic. In the 1960s the Housemaster of Churchill still used the same baths as the boys – his bathing taking place once his charges had departed to class. In the 1970s resident masters in the main building had to wander from one end of the building to the other to have a wash; in the 1980s a resident Housemaster was reprimanded for being extravagant when he suggested a partition might be erected separating his own accommodation from a corridor containing boys' dayrooms. The main school building imposes huge restrictions on the possibilities for family accommodation and this is a difficulty the School continues to confront. The bachelor master who conveniently disappeared during the vacations – once the mainstay of the School – is now a figure of the past although the arrangements of the main building have yet to come to terms with this.

Chapel continues to be a central part of the life of the School although the occasions on which there are formal Sunday Chapel Services are fewer. The early Johnian would have experienced a daily Chapel Service, two Services on Sunday, and House prayers at the end of each day. Into the 1980s there was a weekly Sunday Service. The introduction of fortnightly and then weekly boarding meant changes to Sunday Services with evening Services becoming routine. Today there is a fortnightly Sunday Service for each half of the School and a weekly voluntary Eucharist. During the week the Chapel is as active as it has ever been with five of the six working days beginning there.

If the Johnian at the turn of the nineteenth century glimpsed the Johnian at the turn of the twentieth century there would barely be recognition. The comfort of the Houses, the choice of lunchtime foods, the evening casual clothes, the Student Council, the Sixth Form bar, the satellite television, the small screens being stared at for considerable portions of the day, even the way juniors talk to seniors and, of course, the girls. Yet envy should be tempered. For in many ways the modern Johnian, student and teacher, has more pressures with which to contend. In particular the academic demands are far greater. The appearance of League Tables in the early 1990s imposed huge pressures on schools and the beginning of the culture of comparison and appraisal; schools, departments, teachers, students matched against one another in the name of performance management. This is a new world. There were no formal Heads of Department meetings in the School till the 1980s nor a Director of Studies. Any suggestion of systematically monitoring the academic performance of pupils or departments was dismissed as misleading and unhelpful till the late 1980s. On the pastoral side, too, there has been a transformation of attitudes and demands, creating greater pressure for House staff. The Children Act, the Social Services Inspection, above all the demands and expectations of parents and children have meant a far closer monitoring of pastoral care. Long gone are the days when a boarding Housemaster could be 'on duty' by telephoning his House Captain from an Indian restaurant following a Common Room cricket match.

When Ted Hartwell arrived at St. John's in 1970 he was – like Jack Carter forty years before him – unimpressed with many of the School's facilities. If the School were to compete effectively with its many competitors then its facilities needed to at least be a match for them. A building programme was put in place which has continued with few pauses to the present. Funded by both appeals and surpluses the teaching areas have been transformed. In 1970 the new Biology Laboratory was constructed at the same time as new small seminar classrooms were built into the structure of the existing classroom block. The areas of the School described by the Headmaster as 'squalid, subterranean regions' – the basements of the main building and Blocks A and B – were turned into studies and washing facilities. The huge fifty-bed dormitories at the top of West House and South House were partitioned into smaller units. The old sanatorium, next to the Dining Hall, was removed to the main building releasing space for new Art and Music areas. A new Science department housing Physics and Chemistry was constructed. In 1998 teaching facilities were further enhanced with the new building super-imposed on the front of the classroom block, providing teaching accom-modation, an Information Technology Centre, Sixth Form Study Centre and Multi-Media Studio. At the same time the facilities in the Houses – particularly the boarding Houses – have been further improved. The old fifty-bed dormitories, partitioned into smaller units in the 1970s, have become single study-bedrooms at the turn of the century.

Sporting facilities have improved, too. In 1985 the School purchased

13 acres of land alongside the M25 from Merton College, Oxford – thus creating the New Fields. In 1992 the Sports Hall was built and, into the new century, an astro-turf pitch has been constructed on a section of the Junior Field to provide an all-weather surface and improved recreational facilities for all students but particularly for girls.

As the new millennium gets underway, work is being started on a new Theatre, a Performing Arts complex and Sixth Form Centre, while all the time there are improvements to study and dayroom facilities for both the day and boarding communities. The need to build and improve – a constant theme of the School and the key factor in the decision to move to Leatherhead in 1872 – lives on; it brings huge satisfaction but considerable responsibility. The upward moving spiral of Arthur Rutty continues.

Historians are wary of imposing 'significance' upon events and personalities of the past for this 'significance' might be a consequence of hindsight possessed by the historian but unavailable to the participants; and the historian can make anything 'significant' if he shapes the material in such a way as to justify his claim. Nevertheless, wariness will be put to one side and, by way of conclusion, a few significant events and personalities in the history of St. John's School will be suggested: Ashby Haslewood's letter to his parishioners which began the School; Charles Churchill's seizure of the initiative in 1854; Lewis Mercier – some recognition for the School's most obscure Headmaster – without whom the School almost certainly would have closed in 1857; the Baden Powell family's refusal to allow the School to purchase Clapton House – thus forcing the move to Leatherhead; Arthur Rutty's headmastership; Jack Carter's headmastership; the Field Marshal's interest and involvement in the School; Ted Hartwell's successful drive to attract day boys; the arrival of girls in 1989; the decision in 1992 to await the new Headmaster before embarking upon fundamental changes to the structure of the School. There is probably too much of an emphasis here on the grand and the good – the decision-makers of the School. Thought might be given to the couple of boys who stood watching a military parade on a summer's afternoon in 1948 and who so impressed Viscount Montgomery of Alamein that he gladly gave much of his later life to the well-being of the

School. What if those boys had been a couple of scruffs reeking of nicotine, wandering back from an illicit smoke? Such a concept is barely conceivable of course.

A recurring theme has been mentioned – the constant need to improve and update facilities with the consequent pressure placed upon the School to be financially viable. There is another theme – a deeper one – which runs throughout the story of St. John's: the dynamic tension between the upholders of tradition and, for want of a better term, the pragmatists. It is, of course, possible to be both and the key players in the story have been both. But without this dynamic tension the School would not have survived to continue its work of encouraging its community, governors, staff and students, 'to seek those things which are above.'

The First Pupils of St. John's School
Elected 20ᵗʰ January 1852

Robert Brocklebank. 147 votes

Father 'vicar of a Parish in the diocese of Chichester. He has ten children, nine entirely dependent upon him. His whole income is £100 p.a. of which he has to pay house rent etc., there being no parsonage house. He has been vicar 11 years, and his family is suffering great distress.'

William Lacon. 58 votes

Father 'Perpetual Curate in the Diocese of Worcester. He has seven children, six of whom are dependent upon him; this district is very populous. By great exertion he has lately procured the creation of schools which are very numerously attended by a population reclaimed from dissent; the care of these and of evening schools engrosses his whole time.'

Archibald Hamblin Lillingstone Cole. 50 votes

Father 'incumbent of a district in the diocese of Lichfield. The population nearly 5,000, poor, and engaged in the iron works. He has nine children, eight dependent upon him; the eldest son, aged eighteen, is a cripple, and a daughter, aged seven, also a cripple from her birth. The Father's health is declining from overwork.'

Francis Alexander Robert Morrison. 47 votes

Father 'a clergyman in the diocese of Exeter and Headmaster of an endowed school. He has six children, all dependent upon him, and there is no residence belonging to the school.'

Lionel William Stanton. 44 votes

Father 'incumbent of a very poor and populous district in the diocese of Lichfield; the people are engaged in mining. He has six children, all dependent upon him; the church has been built by his unwearied exertions.'

Arthur Lowndes. 40 votes

Father 'Vicar of a Parish of nearly 3,000 inhabitants in the diocese of Exeter, nearly all poor. He has held the living for twenty-seven years and has three children dependent upon him. He is between sixty and seventy year of age.'

Joseph Hodgson Hilton. Nominated by St. Mark's churchwardens.

Father 'clergyman in the diocese of Bath and Wells; having no permanent employment he is entirely dependent on temporary duty; he has seven children, all dependent upon him, and is in the greatest distress.'

William Henry Wilson. Nominated by Ashby Haslewood.

No details available.

Chairmen of the Governing Body of St. John's School

Before 1875 the committee* appointed a chairman for each meeting; there was no official 'chairman' till then.

1875	J.F. Eastwood
1876	The Revd Sir E.G. Moon
1877–1880	E.H. Lushington
1881–1905	C. Churchill
1905–1908	S. Bircham
1909–1918	The Revd W. Hunt
1918–1930	E.R. Still
1930–1934	H.H. Gordon Clark
1935–1936	F. Hopkins
1937	H.C. King
1937–1947	E.L. Churchill
1947–1950	Sir G. Lloyd Jacob
1950–1966	Viscount Montgomery of Alamein
1966–1979	M.R. Monier-Williams
1980–1984	A.H.C. Greenwood
1985–1997	C.H. Whitby
1997–	M.E. Doherty

* The 'committee' became the 'Council' after 1922.

The Churchill and Gordon Clark Families

Rarely can a school have owed so much to two families. A Churchill and a Gordon Clark have supported the School since its beginning. The 'tree' below gives an idea of the years of service given by members of these families and the manner in which they are interlinked. In time alone their gifts to the School are incomputable. To this must be added their frequent gifts of money. Charles Churchill funded seven of the eight Albany Scholarships and he was also responsible for the building of the library in 1881. More recently the Gordon Clark family has funded a travel bursary for members of the teaching staff. A fifth generation of Gordon Clark currently sits on the School Council. Charles Dawkins, a Gordon Clark cousin, served on the Council between 1956 and 1984.

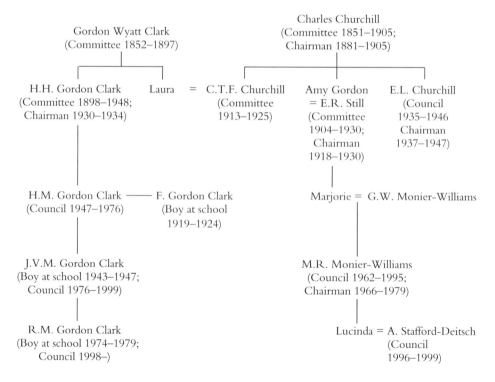

Gordon Wyatt Clark
(Committee 1852–1897)

Charles Churchill
(Committee 1851–1905;
Chairman 1881–1905)

H.H. Gordon Clark
(Committee 1898–1948;
Chairman 1930–1934)

Laura = C.T.F. Churchill
(Committee
1913–1925)

Amy Gordon
= E.R. Still
(Committee
1904–1930;
Chairman
1918–1930)

E.L. Churchill
(Council
1935–1946
Chairman
1937–1947)

H.M. Gordon Clark ——— F. Gordon Clark
(Council 1947–1976)   (Boy at school
1919–1924)

Marjorie = G.W. Monier-Williams

J.V.M. Gordon Clark
(Boy at school 1943–1947;
Council 1976–1999)

M.R. Monier-Williams
(Council 1962–1995;
Chairman 1966–1979)

R.M. Gordon Clark
(Boy at school 1974–1979;
Council 1998–)

Lucinda = A. Stafford-Deitsch
(Council
1996–1999)

Headmasters of St. John's School

Anthony Thomson	1851–1857	Lincoln College, Oxford
Lewis Mercier	1857–1861	University College, Oxford
Edwards Hawkins	1861–1883	Exeter College, Oxford
Arthur Rutty	1883–1909	Pembroke College, Cambridge
Edmund Downes	1909–1932	University College, Oxford
Jack Carter	1933–1947	Balliol College, Oxford
Hereward Wake	1948–1960	Keble College, Oxford
Ian Sutherland	1960–1970	Sidney Sussex College, Cambridge
Edward Hartwell	1970–1985	St. John's College, Oxford
David Brown	1985–1992	Fitzwilliam College, Cambridge
Christopher Tongue	1993–	Jesus College, Cambridge

School Chaplains

(before 1908 many of the teaching staff were ordained;
there was no official chaplain)

1908–1935	The Revd C.W. Ingram
1926–1936	The Revd W.M. Richards
1936–1939	The Revd K.W. Meiklejohn
1938–1940	The Revd G.StL. Hyde Gosselin
1940–1942	The Revd D. Melhuish
1941–1942	The Revd S.M. Minifie-Hawkins
1942–1943	The Rt Revd W.J. Carey
1942–1946	The Revd H.T.G. Forster
1946–1960	The Revd K.W. Meiklejohn
1950–1953	The Revd B.A. Soltau
1954–1964	The Revd J.L. Birley
1960–1964	The Revd C.H.D. Cullingford
1964–1971	The Revd L.M. Cooper
1971–1974	The Revd J.C. Sykes
1974-1983	The Revd A.C. Charters★
1983–1994	The Revd M.R. Francis★
1989–1992	The Revd I.A. Terry
1994–1997	The Revd N. Gosnell
1997–	The Revd M.J. Lawson

★ Was also Deputy Headmaster

The Houses and the Housemasters

Houses were first established in 1892. There were nine of them, founded purely for competitive purposes, and membership depended on from where a pupil originated. The nine original Houses and Housemasters were:

Wales and Montgomery	The Headmaster
West of England	R.T. Milford
London and District	A.F. Fraser Smith
Home Counties	The Reverend C.E. Marsh
East Anglian	The Reverend H.H. Beaumont
East Midland	A.E. Crawley
West Midland	J.T. Knight
North Eastern	J.M. Farrar
North Western	A.J. Dexter

This scheme proved unwieldy and two years later gave way to a simplified system of four Houses still based on the same principle of the place of origin of the pupil.

North	A.E. Crawley
South	A.F. Fraser Smith
East	The Reverend C.E. Marsh
West	The Reverend H.H. Beaumont

The four 'discarded' Housemasters – Messrs. Milford, Knight, Farrar and Dexter all left the School in 1894 when the new system began. The Headmaster gave up his housemastering to concentrate on headmasterly duties.

HOUSEMASTERS AND HOUSEMISTRESSES OF
THE MODERN PERIOD

NORTH

J.D.M.Turner	1953–1965
J.R. Templeman	1965–1980
D.C. Spooner	1980–1987
P.C. Noble	1987–

SOUTH

A.M.S. Clark	1953–1961
D.W. Pitt	1961–1974
J. D. Jones	1974–1989
A.B. Gale+	1989–1993

EAST

T.A.H. Peacocke	1947–1963
H.L. Kennedy	1963–1978
P.K. Smith	1978–1987
B.W. Stevens	1987–2001
S.M. Antwis	2001–

WEST

F.O. Hayden	1945–1966
I. Tomlinson	1966–1981
R.B. Hughes	1981–1996
R.C.B. Clark	1996–

CHURCHILL

G.L. Gettins★	1937–1943
G.L. Crozier	1943–1950
M.B. Shaw	1950–1968
J. Lloyd	1968–1974
S.W. Chubb	1974–1976
B.C. Williams	1976–1992
A.P. King	1992–

SURREY

D.G. Ellis-Jones★	1948–1965
G.T. Evans	1965–1978
D.R. Southion	1978–1990
I. Ruddlesdin	1991–2001
D.F. Parker	2001–

MONTGOMERY

R.D.W. Rhodes★	1973–1975
M.E.C. Comer	1975–1984
A.J. Phillips	1984–1989
P.D. Wells-Cole	1989–1993
A.B. Gale	1993–

HALLATON

T. Rowell★	1989–1993
Mrs. C. Richards	1993–1996
T. Rowell	1996–1999
Ms R. Sullivan	1999–2001
Mrs. J. Porter	2001–

★ First housemaster   + Last housemaster

Bibliography

School and Ecclesiastical Records

St. John's School Minute Books of the Council

St. John's School Reports of the Committee

'The Johnian' Magazine

St. Mark's Church, Hamilton Terrace, Parish Papers

The Blomfield Correspondence Vols. 51 and 53

Fulham Papers – Visitation Returns from St. Mark's, Hamilton Terrace, 1858

Secondary Sources

Blackie, J.	Bradfield, 1850-1975 (1975) *St. Andrew's College*
Blumenau, R.	A History of Malvern College (1965) *Macmillan*
Draper, F.W.M.	Four Centuries of Merchant Taylors' School 1561-1961 (1962) *Oxford University Press*
Hamilton, N.	Monty the Field Marshal (1986) *Hamish Hamilton*
Heeney, B.	Mission to the Middle Classes, the Woodard Schools 1848-1891 (1969) *S.P.C.K.*
Honey, J.R.deS.	Tom Brown's Universe (1977) *Millington*
Hughes, R.B.	St. John's Foundation School (1987) *St. John's School Leatherhead*
Kitson Clark, G.	Churchmen and the Condition of England (1973) *Methuen*
Mallet, C.	Anthony Hope and His Books (1935) *Hutchinson*
Seaman, C.M.E.	Christ's Hospital: the Last Years in London (1977) *Ian Allen Ltd.*
Vardey, E. (ed)	History of Leatherhead (1988) *Leatherhead and District History Society*
Williams, E.M.P.	The Quest Goes On (1951) *St. Johns School, Leatherhead*

Articles

Bamford, T.W.	Public Schoolmasters; a Nineteenth Century Profession (Education and the Professions, 1953)
Healey, E.	Angela Burdett-Coutts (History Today, April 1975)
Power, W.R.	Hackney Schools: a retrospect (Hackney Downs School, 1926)
Serling, L. Kelsey	Education of the Anglican Clergy, 1830-1914 (Leicester University PhD thesis, 1982)
Stuttard, J.	History of Leatherhead, 1986

Index

111